16×12/04 ✓ 4/05
22×7/06 ✓ 5/06
25×8/06 ✓ 9/07
38×7/10 ✓ 11/10

Y PB

Tours FOR FREE™
CALIFORNIA

SOUTHERN CALIFORNIA & LAS VEGAS, NEVADA

Tours FOR FREE™
CALIFORNIA

SOUTHERN CALIFORNIA & LAS VEGAS, NEVADA

WITHDRAWN

BentLight media

Every effort has been made to ensure the completeness and accuracy of all information in this book. However, the information in this book is subject to change at the discretion of the tour operators. It is recommended that you always call ahead when planning tours. Logos, packaging and photographs contained in this edition are either the trademark or copyright of the business that operates the tour. No compensation has been made to the publisher for inclusion of tours in this book. It was the goal of the publisher to include as many free tours in the California area as possible. Inclusion or exclusion of a tour does not imply any editorial or critical statement about any tour.

Bent*Light* Media
© 2002 BentLight Media Inc.
All rights reserved. This book, or any parts thereof, may not be reproduced in any form without permission of the publisher.

Contact:
BentLight Media Inc. 637 S. Broadway B pmb 334 Boulder, Colorado 80305
Phone: 303.543.8532 • Toll Free: 888.851.5778
http://www.ToursForFree.com

Printed in the United States of America

ISBN: 1-893722-03-1

Library of Congress Cataloging-in-Publication Data Jill, Jodi

Tours For Free California: Southern California, Las Vegas, Nevada
1. California - Tours - Handbooks, manuals, etc. 3. Tour guides (Manuals)
4. Manufacturing industries - United States - Directories. 5. Industries - United States - Directories.

Visual Engineering: Mercury Design Group - www.MercuryDG.com
Printed by: Johnson Printing, Boulder, CO

Photo Credits
Front Cover: Taylor Guitar promotional photo, Getty Center and Mission Bells, Andy Miss,
Back Cover: Michelle Maloy Dillon www.mmdphotography.com (Author)

Tours For Free California is available at discount rates for educational, promotional, corporate gift packages, and school fundraisers. Please contact the publisher at info@tourforfree.com or the address and phone numbers above.

Tours *FOR* **FREE**™

TABLE OF CONTENTS

GREATER LOS ANGELES

DOWN TOWN LOS ANGELES

Avila Adobe 3

California Science Center 5

Chapalita Tortilla...6

El Pueblo de Los Angeles...7

Goodwill Industries...8

Grand Central Market 10

La Brea Tar Pits 11

Los Angeles City Hall 12

Los Angeles Farmers Market.....................................13

Los Angeles Performing Arts Theater.......................14

Los Angeles Public Library 15

Los Angeles Times Editorial Tour 17

Los Angeles Times Olympic Plant Tour 18

San Antonio Winery 20

Wells Fargo History Museum 21

HOLLYWOOD AND SAN FERNANDO VALLEY

Frederick's of Hollywood Lingerie Museum...............25

Gordon Howard Museum Complex...........................26

Guide Dogs of America...27

Hollywood Walk of Stars...28

Krispy Kreme Donuts 29

Orcutt Ranch Horticulture Center 30

The Nethercutt Collection 31

The Nethercutt Museum 32

The Road to Hollywood 34

William S. Hart Museum 35

PASADINA AND VICINITY

Bungalow Heaven landmark Tour................................41

Jet Propulsion Laboratory 42

The Old Mill 44

LOS ANGELES COAST

Banning Residence Museum..47

Bell of Friendship 49

Cabrillo Marine Aquarium 50

Casa de Tortuga...51

Crystal Cathedral...53

Drum Barracks Civil War Museum.................................54

Getty Center 56

Long Beach Airport 57

Los Angeles Maritime Museum 58

Los Angeles Temple..59

Lummis House...60

Marine Mammal Care Center at Fort MacArthur 61

Rancho Los Alamitos 62

Wayfarers Chapel...64

CENTRAL COAST

Channel Islands Mainland Visitors Center 67

El Presidio de Santa Barbara 69

Fillmore Fish Hatchery...70

Karpeles Manuscript Library Museum 71

Olivas Adobe 72

Oxnard Heritage Square..73

Red Tile Tour..74

Santa Barbara Airport 75

Santa Barbara County Courthouse..76

Santa Barbara Historical Museum 77

Santa Barbara Winery 78

Ventura Historic Walking Tour...79

Witch Creek Winery 80

INLAND EMPIRE

California Museum of Photography..83

Fleetwood RV 85

Graber Olive House..86

Historical Glass Museum...88

Lincoln Memorial Shrine 89

March AFB Field Museum 90

SilverCrest Homes..91

Workman and Temple Family Homestead Museum.................93

ORANGE COUNTY

Heritage Hill Historical Park 97

Orange County Performing Arts Center.....................................98

Orange County Register...99

SOUTHERN COAST

Antique Gas and Steam Engine Museum..................................103

Bates Nut Farm..105

Bell Gardens 106

Buena Vista Audubon Nature Center..107

California Surf Museum 108

Callaway Golf (ball tour) 109

Callaway Golf (club tour)...110

Lawrence Welk Museum 112

National RV Factory Tour 114

Orfila Vineyards..115

Taylor Made Adidus Golf 116

Winchester Cheese 118

SAN DIEGO COUNTY

Arco Olympic Center..121

Balboa Park 123

Bernardo Winery 126

Buck Knives 124

Hotel del Coronado 127

Museum of Contemporary Art Downtown...............128

Old Town San Diego State Historical Park 129

Salk Institute for Biological Studies 131

San Diego Mineral and Gem Society 132

San Diego Union Tribune..133

Summers Past Farms 135

Taylor Guitars..136

The Timken Museum of Art 137

Wells Fargo History Museum 138

HIGH DESERT

China Ranch 141

LAS VEGAS, NEVADA

Atlantis Aquarium Behind the Scenes Tour...............145

Ethel M. Chocolates...147

Flamingo Hilton Wildlife Habitat..............................149

Lion Habitat 150

McCarran Aviation History Museum...151

National Vitamin Company 152

Ron Lee's World of Clowns..153

Shelby Car Company 154

FREE DAYS & EVENTS

Down Town Los Angeles 157

Hollywood & San Fernando 158

Pasadena & Vicinity 159

Los Angeles Coast 161

Inland Empire 166

Orange County 166

Central Coast 168

San Diego 170

Las Vegas, Nevada 178

Tours FOR FREE™ CALIFORNIA

SOUTHERN CALIFORNIA & LAS VEGAS, NEVADA

INTRODUCTION

With only a short drive, you can find an experience of Southern California that will gratify your soul. Whether exploring the mountain ranges that poke into the sky or laying at the base of the earth that flows into the ocean, you will enjoy Southern California. People who live in this diverse area know the importance of both regions and the spaces in-between. The special relationship Southern California has with her residents can be matched by no other region. The residents, culturally diverse and proud of their heritage, open their arms sharing all they have to offer and in turn live well.

The commerce of Southern California is equally impressive. Creating goods and services enjoyed around the world, some of the nation's leading companies are found in this area. From ground breaking new technology to helping people and the natural environment of Southern California these tours show off the best the state has to offer.

As in the past, Southern California will continue to be a leader in creative and innovative contributions to the world. The tours in this book will give a taste of this wonderful state to all those who venture to explore.

Enjoy your free tours!

Jodi Jill

NOTE FROM THE PUBLISHER

Welcome to the next edition of Tours For Free. This series of books is dedicated to everyone who loves to explore and discover more about a region than what is commonly found on the typical vacation. The tours offered by companies, private groups, foundations, and government agencies are not only great because they are free, but because they offer an experience of the real people that live in the region. By exploring what is made and how people work, a new appreciation can be gained for the "who," "why" and "how" of a region instead of just the "what to see." These tours are entertaining and educational, making most of them perfect for children.

All of us at *BentLight Media* love free tours almost as much as we love making quality books, so if you have any comments about our books or suggestions for additional tours, we want to hear from you.

John Kellow, Publisher

HOW TO USE THIS BOOK

To make it easy to find tours in the area you are interested in exploring, Tours For Free Southern California is laid out in seven different regions with an eighth region for the Las Vegas, Nevada area. Within each region, cities are listed alphabetically and the tours within these cities are listed alphabetically by name. If you are looking for a specific tour, reference the index in the back of the book.

THE ART OF TOURING

TIPS *Here are a few basic tips to make your touring experience the very best!*

■ Before attending a tour call the facility to check the schedule, find out any additional directions and clarify any details that will be necessary for the tour to be enjoyable. The information in this book is current as of our publication date, but we can not guarantee that it will not change.

■ Wear comfortable clothes and shoes while touring and layer your clothing to adjust for an unexpected temperature change. Some tours have dress codes, so check it out before you go.

■ Don't bring too many items you will need to carry during the tour. Keep what you bring to a minimum.

■ Check with the tour guide to find out if it is permissible to take pictures during the tour. Certain companies will not allow photographs to be taken.

■ Most tours will make children feel special and welcome. Call ahead if you are unsure.

■ Stroller requirements will vary, so if you have a smaller child call ahead to find out if there are any space limitations.

■ Be on time for a scheduled tour! If you are going to be late, call the facility to let them know. They may accommodate your unexpected delay or reschedule the tour.

■ If you have any questions, ask the tour guide. Keep in mind that they may not have every answer, but most will make arrangements to find the answer if possible.

■ Stay with your tour group and ask the tour guide before touching anything.

■ Every tour guide will provide the best possible setting for a safe and enjoyable tour, but there are hazards. If you understand the risks and stay alert, you will reduce your chances of getting hurt or damaging equipment.

- Be modest when taking samples. If you would like more, you can always ask after the tour is over.

- Ask for more information! Some facilities will provide brochures at the end of the tour.

- When the tour is complete, take a moment to thank your tour guide. If they did an outstanding job, you should consider sending a card to thank them or let their supervisor know how impressed you were.

- When touring you need to roll with the punches. If you didn't get the chance to see what you wanted, try again. Remember that the tours are part of a larger operation.

- Many of the facilities listed have gift shops. While you are under no obligation to buy anything, you will have the chance to purchase one-of-a-kind items in these shops.

TAKING SELF-GUIDED TOURS

Some people might prefer to consume knowledge at their own speed, or perhaps they do not like crowds. No problem! There are listings for self-guided tours so you can explore Southern California at your own pace.

A self-guided tour will not give you the added feature of asking an experienced individual to share their knowledge, but you will still learn plenty. Displays, interactive computers, and photographs will be available. It is important to call the facility to confirm a self-guided tour, especially if the location is far from home.

TAKING GUIDED TOURS

The tour guides in Southern California are pleasant people who will try to accommodate your requests. Whether touring alone, with family or as part of a class, your request will be handled with the same enthusiasm that guides share during the tour. When you call the facility to schedule a tour, it is a good idea to have the following information ready to share:

1. Age range and number of people attending
2. Amount of time that is needed to tour
3. Any special requirements or concerns (e.g. wheelchairs, strollers, people who have difficulty walking long distances, people who are allergic to certain chemicals)
4. Two or three dates and times when the group could conveniently tour

If you are unable to attend the scheduled tour call the facility and let the tour guide know. They will appreciate the call and you will be able to reschedule for a later date. It is also important to let the facility know if the number of people in your group changes, as many tours have guidelines regarding how many people are in each group. Keep in mind that a facility might need to cancel a tour, so it is advisable to call and confirm on the day of the tour.

THE EDUCATOR AND SOUTHERN CALIFORNIA TOURS

Taking children on tours, whether as school groups, home school families or extra curricular organizations, is a fabulous way to explore and learn! You will give children an experience that will encourage them to ask questions and a wonderful opportunity to discover Southern California.

Before calling to schedule a tour, there are a few important details to clarify:

- The number of students attending and their age range
- How the tour will create or enhance the classroom work
- Any special needs or concerns
- Length of time needed for the tour
- Convenient dates for the tour

Once the tour guide knows this information they can help decide if their tour would be appropriate for your group. Usually the tour guide will schedule a group tour as a top priority, especially for education. Many of the facilities will provide worksheets and scavenger hunt activity guides that will compliment children's touring experience. Most of the educational tours will offer free items to children, Such as book markers, rulers, pencils, and information packets. These little items excite children and encourage them to pay attention to the tour's message. Once you have secured a date, talk with the tour guide to find out what they have to offer. The children will thank you a million times.

TOURING VINEYARDS AND WINERIES

Fruit is one of the most precious commodities in California, especially grapes. While Napa Valley is known as a Mecca for vineyards and wineries, Southern California holds its own with many fine vineyards and wineries. From Santa Barbara to San Diego, these vineyards and wineries produce quality wines for the community. While many of the wineries charge for tours and tasting, those listed in this book are all free.

Touring wineries is both entertaining and educational. From the flowery terminology to the fermentation process, visitors leave with a new understanding of one of the oldest beverages known to man. When you are deciding where to tour, an important aspect to consider is the difference between vineyards, wineries and cellars. A vineyard is where the grapes are grown and wine is made. The vineyard might be in its first or fifth year, but no matter how mature the crop, there will be grapes growing on the property. A winery is called such because the wines are made from grapes that are shipped to the facility from another location. By using the term cellars, a company implies that both a winery and a vineyard are on the property, and the harvest used for the wine production is from their vineyard. No matter which tour you decide to take, all of the wineries listed in this book use California grapes.

Another important term to remember is vintner. He or she is the central figure in the winery, the wine maker. The number of vintners depends on the type of wine they highlight and the number of gallons produced annually.

Depending on the time of the year and how many visitors are in your group, wineries and vineyards welcome guests to view their premises and enjoy their tasting rooms. It is advisable to call ahead to set an appointment. This will allow you to confirm business hours or perhaps arrange a private tour and tasting. The actual time for the winemaking tour will only be ten or fifteen minutes. It will include some history of the business and a basic tour to look at the equipment and facilities. You will enjoy absorbing information about the winemaking process from the vintner. Ask plenty of questions on the tour and you will become a wine aficionado before you leave. The time allotted for the tour will be somewhat limited, but there should be plenty of time for tasting the wines and enjoying the views. Tasting rooms vary as each vintner puts together a room that compliments their wine. A large selection of wine will be on display in the tasting rooms, and you will be welcome to try a free sample. Some of the tasting rooms feature elegant food items that are for sale, while others highlight wine related products such as corkscrews. Logo merchandise is available at many of the wineries, and you will always find cases upon cases of wine available for purchase. Most of the tasting rooms have outdoor seating, so you can pull up a chair and relax while you sample the wine. If you decide to bring a picnic, you could buy a bottle of your favorite wine to accompany the meal.

LEVEL OF DIFFICULTY

Tours For Free uses an easy to understand rating system for the level of difficulty for each tour. These ratings are helpful to ensure that you have the best possible time on the tour. If you are concerned about a specific tour, you can always call ahead.

EASY: On these tours you can expect a short walk without any climbing of stairs.

Moderate: On these tours you can expect a longer walk with some climbing of stairs or hills.

Difficult: On these tours you can expect to walk a significant distance, with stairs or hills to climb.

Tours FOR FREE™

AVILA ADOBE

CALIFORNIA SCIENCE CENTER

CHAPALITA TORTILLA

EL PUEBLO DE LOS ANGELES

GOODWILL INDUSTRIES

GRAND CENTRAL MARKET

LA BREA TAR PITS

LOS ANGELES CITY HALL

LOS ANGELES FARMERS MARKET

LOS ANGELES
PERFORMING ARTS THEATER

LOS ANGELES PUBLIC LIBRARY

LOS ANGELES TIMES
EDITORIAL TOUR

LOS ANGELES TIMES
OLYMPIC PLANT TOUR

SAN ANTONIO WINERY

WELLS FARGO
HISTORY MUSEUM

DOWNTOWN LA

AVILA ADOBE

The oldest house standing in Los Angeles is the Avila Adobe, located only one block from downtown. Built by the Avila family in 1818, the house now rests in the middle of the El Pueblo de Los Angeles Historic Monument on Olvera Street.

Sparsely furnished, the rooms at the Adobe are reflective of the California lifestyle in the 1840's. Walking through each room connected by a hallway, guests are able to see the essentials of the time. The coolness of the air inside the adobe is from the thick dirt slabs that make the walls of the house. Submerged in the private home of the Avila family, visitors have an opportunity to walk through the house and capture a glimpse of the past. The home gives a vivid sense of what family farm life was like over 100 years ago and the rich details make this a captivating tour.

Successful ranchers and traders of cowhides and tallow, the Avilas were known for their generosity and kindness and many prominent guests visited their home. Among the famous visitors was Jedediah Smith, the first non-native American to enter California overland from the east and the first to cross the enormous Great Basin Desert and return east, overland from California.

The adobe tour begins in the formally appointed family room where the Avilas entertained their many guests. Just off the family room is the office where day-to-

TAKE THE TOUR

WHERE TO GO
El Pueblo de Los Angeles
Historic Monument
125 Paseo de la Plaza
Los Angeles, CA 90012

WHEN TO GO
Self-Guided Tours
Guided Tours
9am - 3pm
Guided Tours on the Hour

DEGREE OF DIFFICULTY
Easy

CONTACT
213.628.1274

day business was managed. Original papers, ledgers and office equipment are here, just as if the clerk had stepped away for a moment. These records of commerce are silent testimony to the influential Avila family who played an important role in the development of commerce in Los Angeles.

The tour includes stops in the period kitchen, bedroom, and sitting room. The last room on the home tour is the children's room where replica straw mattresses and trunks for their clothes are among the furnishings. Leaving the house, you enter the courtyard where "running" water was provided via a small ditch.

Two other exhibits at the home provide additional context to the commercial and social evolution of the City of Angels. Water In Los Angeles is a timeline exhibit that shows the different ways this vital resource was imported to the growing city. The early photographs show the geographic changes in the methods of water delivery and the changes in its use over the past 50 years.

The second exhibit tells the story of Christine Sterling, the woman responsible for saving the Avila Adobe from being condemned. Los Angeles declared the site unsafe as the house was badly damaged and planed to demolish it. Mrs. Sterling worked actively to restore the area and convert it into an educational and historical area. The permanent exhibit honoring her efforts end the tour and can be found on the path back to the Olvera Street Plaza.

CALIFORNIA SCIENCE CENTER

The California Science Center, only five miles from downtown Los Angeles is a great place to explore the science of life and commerce. With its inspiring scientific works and gadgets, the entire center is a great place to learn about the world and the universe. Most of the exhibits are interactive, giving the kids lots to touch and play with.

As visitors enter the building, the hyperbolic paraboloid hangs overhead. The 5,000 pound kinetic sculpture grows from a cluster to an image five stories high. This captivating installation is visible from every floor, offering a different perspective as it moves.

Starting on the second floor, The World of Life is the first gallery to explore. Following the processes of all living things from single cell animals to a human, visitors will see the biological basis of the world. As visitors walk through the area, there is a lot to see and even more to miss if you're not careful. The California Science Center has used every inch of space, including the ceiling, for exhibits.

Near the entrance, take time to get a good look at the Cell Lab. There are microscopes with which to peer into the active world of single-cell creatures. Near the Cell Lab is the Energy Factory display, a fun food-oriented exhibit that will make lunchtime a learning exercise. The entire human digestive track is shown and kids will really get a kick out of the "growling" of the digestive track.

The technology of today is the focus of the remainder of the second floor and most of the third. From earthquake safety in buildings to digital imaging, there is a lot to see and do. A particularly fun, interactive exhibit on the third floor is the aerodynamics lesson. Standing in front of a large fan, visitors get to see how airplanes and sail boats make use of wind and air to create lift and propulsion. In the far back corner the Technoscapes images _ lifelike sculpture displays made from plaster molds – show how humans benefit from modern technology. By examining these figures, visitors can see first hand how technology has changed the way we live.

On the way out, a 13-foot granite sculpture pays tribute to the state of California. Making dramatic use of positive and negative space, two cut-out granite rocks comprise the outline of the state. Below, 74 different squares lead visitors along a path of discovery: from riddles to quotes, to number games and images, all relate to science in our world today.

TAKE THE TOUR

WHERE TO GO
700 State Drive
Los Angeles, CA 90037

WHEN TO GO
Self Guided Tour
10am – 5pm Daily

DEGREE OF DIFFICULTY
Moderate

CONTACT
323.724.3623
www.casciencectr.org

TAKE THE TOUR

WHERE TO GO
1815 North Main Street
Los Angeles, CA 90031

WHEN TO GO
Self-Guided Tours
9am to 6pm Daily

DEGREE OF DIFFICULTY
Easy

CONTACT
213.221.0400

CHAPALITA TORTILLERIA

For a tour that your taste buds will enjoy, Chapalita Tortillas offers a simple look at how tortillas are made. Handmade as they have been for generations, these melt-in-your-mouth tortillas put store bought products to shame. The actual location of the company is in the Grand Central Market. The tortillas are primarily made in the morning so visitors will want to arrive early to see the tortilla making process and save exploring the market for later.

The huge machine that makes the tortilla can be seen through a glass partition at the entrance. Although it is huge and ugly, the machine produces quality tortillas famous throughout Los Angeles.

The ingredients of the tortillas are mixed together by hand on a table behind the actual tortilla maker. Big bowls of the mixture are placed on the top of the tortilla machine. Moving toward the middle of the machine, the dough is mixed further and flattened. From there, round cutters slice the dough to make uncooked tortilla flats. Going through the oven in the middle, the dough is cooked to perfection. On the other side, the cooked rounds are placed on a cooling sheet. The sheet, going from side to side, drops five stories before finally ending up on a table.

Cooked, cooled and ready to go, the tortillas are counted and placed in bags. Most of the tortillas produced here are sold at the Grand Central Market and other local venues, meeting the steady demand for these fresh products.

EL PUEBLO DE LOS ANGELES

TAKE THE TOUR

WHERE TO GO
125 Paseo de la Plaza
Los Angeles, CA 90012

WHEN TO GO
Self-Guided Tours
Guided Tours
Tuesday - Saturday
10am-3pm on the hour

DEGREE OF DIFFICULTY
Easy

CONTACT
213.628.1274
www.ci.la.ca.us/ELP/dir.htm

Only a few blocks from the Los Angeles City Hall is the birthplace of the city: El Pueblo De Los Angeles. Founded in 1781, the original 44 settlers of Los Angeles made their home here. Throughout the years, as the town grew, the center moved southward. This 44-acre site surrounding the Old Plaza is a State Historic Park.

The tour begins at the center of the plaza in front of the statue of Felipe De Neve, the first Spanish governor of California who was responsible for founding the city. The tour then focuses on the Pobladores Plaque commemorating the founding settlers. Their names and ethnic origins are listed. A short distance further is the Placita De Dolores, a replica of the Bell that commemorates Mexico's independence from Spain.

The Buildings on this tour are quite fascinating. The Plaza Substation, built by Henry E. Huntington was one of 14 power-generating stations in Los Angeles. The huge system converted electricity from AC to DC for the Electric Red Cars. The Red Cars were a network of rail lines and electric street cars used in the 1920s. The Biscailuz Building – originally the United Methodist Church Conference Headquarters – now houses the Mexican Consulate-General. In the center of the plaza is the Avila Adobe (See tour on page 3). Built in 1818, this is the oldest existing house in Los Angeles. Originally owned by Don Francisco, the house was built for his family but included space for guests of the ranch.

The Mother Ditch or Zanja Madre was the first water system for the pueblo. It is commemorated on Olvera Street by the display of diagonal bricking on the sidewalks. The nine branches of the Zanja Madre served the water needs of the Los Angeles area until the system was abandoned in 1904.

TAKE THE TOUR

WHERE TO GO
342 San Fernando Road
Los Angeles, CA 90031

WHEN TO GO
Guided Tours
Reservations Required

DEGREE OF DIFFICULTY
Easy

CONTACT
323.223.1211
www.lagoodwill.org

GOODWILL INDUSTRIES OF SOUTHERN CALIFORNIA

Goodwill Stores are scattered throughout Southern California. Renowned for great bargains on used merchandise and clothing, the chance to get a great deal on that cool bowling shirt is right inside the door. Goodwill Industries does much more for neighborhoods than provide bargains. Focusing on the special needs of members of the community, the tour at the main facility offers a bigger picture of the organization's mission. It is an unselfish side that involves the community beyond the thrift stores.

Goodwill's main objective is to help those who need assistance in finding jobs or developing job skills. The tour of the main facility goes into many different opportunities Goodwill makes available to the people they serve. One thing visitors will immediately notice on the tour is the community spirit found at Goodwill. Smiles, greetings and the pure kindness extended are unmatched by any other tour found in this book.

The tour takes visitors through the different building levels where it provides people a chance to learn skills and apply those to future jobs. Some of the "classrooms" include restaurant training in a public cafeteria. Others include the cleaning classroom, which looks a bit odd with all the different tiles on the floor. Gaining experience on the tiles, the students are exposed to the various types they will be faced with on the job. Again using these skills immediately, all the people in this program clean the building and based on how spotless it is, they are all getting an A+.

There is a large job facility where community members can use resources of Goodwill to find jobs. With access to computers, printers, telephones and other essential tools, a person can find a job in a stable, supportive setting. Also available are people within different agencies who can help find the perfect job for the applicants.

There is a great deal of effort put into helping individuals with special needs. One important way that Goodwill makes a difference is through the purchase of special equipment to help people with disabilities. By matching individuals with the tools they need to integrate into the work force, they are able to find work with employers that might not have been able to afford the needed equipment that would enable an employer to hire someone with a disability. Removing these barriers to entry in the

workforce opens up a whole new world for hundreds of thankful people. There are many disabilities and problems with which regular people need assistance and Goodwill is one place anyone can turn for help.

The tour also stops at the Goodwill High School, founded to give those students who find themselves with special concerns the opportunity to work in an untraditional learning environment. The students have access to computer labs as well as opportunities not normally found in traditional classroom settings.

Highlighting job skills, Goodwill has contracts with different companies to directly connect students with jobs. Visitors to a dollar store will have seen some of the work by Goodwill. Also, they have contracts with department stores to supply them with hundreds of reused hangers for clothing.

The tour ends at the thrift shop right outside the main building of Goodwill. This is a chance to take a break for lunch at the public cafeteria (they have great food) and see if there is a good deal at the thrift shop.

TAKE THE TOUR

WHERE TO GO
317 South Broadway
Los Angeles, CA 90013

WHEN TO GO
Self-Guided Tour
9am to 6pm daily

DEGREE OF DIFFICULTY
Easy

CONTACT
213.624.2378
www.grandcentralsquare.com

EXTRA INFO
Great for Children and
School Groups

GRAND CENTRAL MARKET

A staple of Los Angeles' shopping experience since 1917, the Grand Central Market is a place to see what old time markets looked like. There are more than 30 places to buy food and other extras – from lunch to produce to take home – and plenty to look at and learn. The Grand Central Market is the focal point of the region of Los Angeles known as the Historic Core District. In addition to being a great place to shop, the market is famous for the offices of the famous architect Frank Lloyd Wright in the space above the main shopping area.

Starting on the Hill Street entrance, the market's charm is immediately apparent. Basic chairs and tables are found in the corners with sawdust spread over the aisles dividing the vendor stalls. As visitors head down the stairs toward Broadway they get the chance to see why the market is so famous. What visitors can't see at this point, they will smell – fresh produce, cooked meats and spices combine to give the senses a feast.

A basic necessity found here is fresh produce. Vendors have boxes of produce lined full of different fruits and vegetables. Scales, all sizes, are hung around for customers to weigh their purchases. One thing that captures the Grand Central of the past is the hand written signs that display the specials each vendor offers.

In the middle of the market is Valeria's. Here mounds of red chilies and cooking spices from all over the world can be purchased by the pound. Nearby, several small, specialty butchers offer everything from beef tongue to pork in quantities ranging from single servings to whole sides of beef.

Next to the spice shop is the famous La Chapalita Tortilla Company. When the market opens, visitors will see how they make and package tortillas. However looking at the stacking racks on the machine, with or without food, gives a good idea of the volume of tortillas they make.

LA BREA TAR PITS

There was a time when dinosaurs walked the face of the earth and many of them ended up in Los Angeles. At the La Brea Tar Pits, scientists excavate bones and artifacts in a search of the origins of life on earth. There are many pits at La Brea including Pit 91 where archeologists are actively excavating specimens.

Located in a small park, visitors know they are in the right place when they get out of the car and smell the goop. The tar pits smell just like the stuff construction workers put on roads or roofs. If visitors find chemical smells offensive, it is suggested that they bring something to cover their nose.

The walk around the tar pits start at the big pit in front of the museum. Here, a wooly mammoth is rising out of the middle of the pit. Around the beast, gas bubbles up through the tar.

Behind the museum are more pits, including Pit 91. This working pit has a fence around it, so getting a complete view is difficult. Buckets and trowels are the only tools used to dig in the pit and, although they may seem a bit simplistic, the archeologists use great care not to use heavy machinery for fear they might damage a valuable specimen.

On the far side of Pit 91 there is a cage that provides a better look inside the pit. Walking into observation area, it is possible to see how the pit is excavated and more details on the history of the excavation.

Three other pits are only steps away from Pit 91. Each pit has facts and figures about the excavation and the discoveries made here. Also posted on the fences is a map to make sure visitors don't miss any secrets hidden in the goop.

TAKE THE TOUR

WHERE TO GO
5801 Wilshire Blvd
Los Angeles, CA 90036

WHEN TO GO
Self-Guided Tour
Sunrise to Sunset
Seven days a week

DEGREE OF DIFFICULTY
Moderate

LOS ANGELES CITY HALL

In downtown Los Angeles, it is difficult to miss the Los Angeles City Hall. Bold and bright white, this building has been the center of the city since 1928. The tour of City Hall gives guests a chance to understand how the government works as well as some history.

Before taking the tour, it is worth a short walk around the grounds to get a good look at the architecture. As with most government buildings, visitors will need to pass through security to start the tour, which begins near the mayor's office on the third floor. From here visitors are shown the murals and gifts given to the City of Los Angeles by visiting dignitaries. The volunteer tour guides are proud of their city and enjoy their jobs as can be seen in their enthusiastic and insightful tours.

A couple of places to pay close attention are the third floor and the elevators. The third floor has a distinct beauty to it. Highlighting art and culture from the past, the murals jump out at the viewer with delightful images and impressions. The special attention given to details on this floor is absolutely amazing. Do check out the gifts displayed. Special displays are made for each piece in honor of the gift recipient. The elevators, in Art Deco style bring visitors back to when the building was first built.

In the style of Hollywood, Los Angeles City Hall is more than just a building used for city government; it has been used as a backdrop for dozens of movies and television shows. After taking this tour, visitors will be surprised at how often it shows up on the television and the big screen.

TAKE THE TOUR

WHERE TO GO
201 North Spring Street
Los Angeles, CA 90012

WHEN TO GO
Guided Tour
Reservations Required

DEGREE OF DIFFICULTY
Easy

CONTACT
213.978.1995
www.ci.la.ca.us

LOS ANGELES FARMERS MARKET

TAKE THE TOUR

WHERE TO GO
6333 West Third Street
Los Angeles, CA 90036

WHEN TO GO
Self Guided Tours
Monday - Friday 9am - 9pm
Saturday 9am - 8pm
Sunday 10am - 7pm

DEGREE OF DIFFICULTY
Easy

CONTACT
323.933.9211
www.farmersmarketla.com

Located next to the CBS Studios on the corner of Third Avenue and Fairfax, the L.A. Farmers Market is a fun place to tour and see how things are made. From ice cream to peanut butter, this tour shows visitors firsthand how the food they eat is made.

A Los Angeles fixture for more than 67 years, the market has an international flavor that enriches the experience of eating cheese, crepes and other goodies to eat. Full of vendors, visitors can find great produce deals, look at gorgeous flowers, enjoy some free samples or just people watch.

Each of the vendors inside the market highlights a specialty. From an entire three-sided case of different kinds of cheese to a shop full of hot sauce, there is something for everyone. On the East side of the market, you can watch as Bennett's Homemade Ice Cream employees make more than five flavors Bennett's makes ice cream every day, usually in the afternoons.

Another place to explore is Magee's Nut House on the south side of the Market. Here visitors can see how peanut butter is made with their "super duper machine" on the corner of their counter. More than five pounds of nuts are set on the top of the grinding machine and steadily poured into the grinder to be turned into a delicious butter. Peanuts aren't the only nuts crushed here, cashew butter is offered as well.

The Farmers Market will soon open a new section of the market called The Grove at Farmers Market. The new facility will house more of the modern chains and big name stores, but don't fear, the old Farmers Market area will remain the agricultural and cultural experience it has for over 67 years.

LOS ANGELES PERFORMING ARTS THEATER

Before the curtain goes up and the actors, dancers or musicians take the stage, there is an entire production that makes it all possible. The tour of the Los Angeles Performing Arts Theater offers a glimpse into the production behind the production.

The tour starts at the Dorothy Chandler Pavilion. Outside, next to the ticket windows, visitors will find a sign where the tours gather at designated times. The tour lasts around 45 minutes and requires walking a flight of steep stairs. They are guided by a small group of volunteers called the Symphonians – mostly women who know a great deal about the theater.

The first stop on the tour is the lobby where a presentation is given about the contributors who funded the center. The company that runs the theater is a non-profit corporation and depends on the donations of benefactors around the city, as well as the volunteers who help ensure that the show will go on.

TAKE THE TOUR

WHERE TO GO
135 North Grand Street
Los Angeles, CA 90012

WHEN TO GO
Guided Tour
Reservations Required

DEGREE OF DIFFICULTY
Moderate

CONTACT
213.972.7211

The next part of the tour includes theater seating. There is a lot more that goes into where each seat is placed than meets the eye. The entire theater was designed to ensure the best sound possible. Combining different woods and placing them in particular positions affects the way sounds are absorbed or reflected. This explanation of the art of acoustics is a fascinating part of the tour.

The balcony provides a higher vantage point of the stage and a chance to see many of the elements of the theater that are not as obvious when all the seats are full. On the outside of the theater, as the tour passes some of the bars, the guide will explain some of the art on the walls.

Back outside, the tour guide talks more about the artwork and the other theaters in the complex. If there is time, it is possible to visit the other theaters in the complex.

LOS ANGELES PUBLIC LIBRARY

The Los Angeles Public Library opened in 1872 and was moved six times before settling in its current location in 1926. The library shelves offer more than 6 million books and 160,000 videos. The tour teaches you much more than where to find information or how to check out a book.

The tour begins in front of the Library Store in the main lobby where you can see the two different buildings that make up the library. The Goodhue Building is the historic side and was connected to the new Tom Bradley Wing in 1993 after renovations were completed.

The best example of the architecture of the Goodhue Building is found on the second floor. Here, four wall size murals each depict a time in the history of California and the Los Angeles area. The murals were started in London and finished in Los Angeles. The colors, while faded over time, give a nostalgic feeling that represents history in the making.

Other interesting works of art found in the Goodhue Building are the murals in the Children's Room and the Catalog Card Drawers stuck into the walls. There are so many works of art on the tour, visitors could easily come back and spend more

TAKE THE TOUR

WHERE TO GO
630 West Fifth Street
Los Angeles, CA 90071

WHEN TO GO
Guided Tours
Monday - Friday 12:30pm
Saturday 11am & 2pm
Sunday 2pm

DEGREE OF DIFFICULTY
Moderate

CONTACT
213.228.7168
www.lapl.org

time looking at each piece in detail.

The Tom Bradley Building, named for the mayor who served from 1973 to 1993, is where most of the book stacks are located. Divided into seven departments, the 8-story building has four levels above ground and four below.

One of the more striking features of the Bradley Building is the chandeliers. The figurines each weigh 1,750 pounds and represent the three areas of information patrons look for in the Library. Before the tour, take a minute and try to figure out what each figure represents. The best place to view these works of art is from the balcony at the far end of the library.

A must-see part of this tour is the elevator. A unique collage using old card catalog cards covers the inside of the elevator. The yellowed cards all begin with 'complete' or 'comprehensive.' Also, as would be expected in the movie capital of the world, there is an extensive video selection.

The library has an excellent garden that is an ideal place to take a break. There are interesting garden pools and sculptures with a walking path. These gardens have been preserved to retain the original beauty of the gardens when they were created in 1926. On the steps up to the library, the evolution of language is depicted. Starting from the earliest cave drawings to the most recent computer code, each step becomes a progressive history lesson in communication. The last step is left blank for the language of the future.

LOS ANGELES TIMES EDITORIAL TOUR

TAKE THE TOUR

WHERE TO GO
201 West 1st Street
Los Angeles, CA 90012

WHEN TO GO
Guided Tours
Reservations Required

DEGREE OF DIFFICULTY
Easy

CONTACT
213.237.5000
www.latimes.com

The Los Angeles Times is the largest newspaper in California with more than 1 million copies printed daily. This figure is made even more astounding by the fact that on most days the newspaper has more than 100 pages, making it one of the thickest newspapers printed. The tour of the editorial section of the newspaper gives visitors an idea of the time and work required to produce a paper of that size every day, from story idea to preproduction.

Giving visitors a general idea of how the newspaper works, the tour guide explains the different sections of the newspaper and its importance of advertising. Open to questions, this tour is great for those interested in the world of media and journalism or anyone who wants to be amazed at how such a complex process can meet a deadline every day.

The tour begins with the travel, books and lifestyle section. The tour guide gives a basic idea on how an idea for a story is generated and the progression into a newspaper article. In this area there is also the opportunity to see the travel library.

When you get to the photography department, don't forget to check out the case with the antique cameras and photographic equipment. Another great thing to see is the wet napkin collection in the California Reporter area. Lined on a column, there are more than 50 different wet napkins – all unopened – from all over the world.

An unexpected feature of the tour is the test kitchen. There are large windows from which to watch chefs preparing meals and desserts for the Wednesday food section. This modern kitchen would be the envy of any chef. The food prepared in the kitchen is ultimately photographed. Unfortunately, they don't give out samples and after sitting under the lights for an hour, the food probably wouldn't taste as good as it looks.

The archives and the library is where reporters and employees of the Los Angeles Times access reference materials. The archives contain the older newspaper articles that were cut out and filed in small envelopes by subject. Today, the archiving system is largely stored on computers.

Visitors will want to keep their eyes open for the amazing photographs that line the hallways and hang in different areas. Most are framed and feature a look into life across the country.

LOS ANGELES TIMES PRINTING PLANT

The Los Angeles Times is one of the largest newspapers in the country. With more than 1 million copies in circulation daily, the process of printing the newspaper is elaborate. The opportunity to see how huge rolls of newsprint are made into a newspaper is a tour not to miss.

TAKE THE TOUR

WHERE TO GO
2000 East 8th Street
Los Angeles, CA 90021

WHEN TO GO
Guided Tours
Reservations Required

DEGREE OF DIFFICULTY
Moderate

CONTACT
213.237.5000
www.latimes.com

Starting in the foyer, visitors will have a chance to see a small press used to print the Los Angeles Times in its early years. Using block letters, each paper was hand printed until all were finished. The blue, computer controlled presses behind the antique machine are four stories tall and as long as a football field.

During this tour it is important to keep in mind that the newspaper is printed in sections. For example, the Sunday travel section might be printed on Wednesday and stacked to be inserted later in the week. Usually the paper is printed backwards with the front section printed last as the editorial content needs to be the most current and has a 10 p.m. deadline.

The tour begins by explaining how robots are programmed to move rolls of paper into place for loading on the printer. From the paper warehouse next door, the newsprint is moved to the bottom of the presses and loaded onto the press and through the rollers. The warehouse room is an awesome sight. At least 100 rolls of

paper, weighing from 1,500 to 2,000 pounds each, are stacked to the ceiling. Moved by a specially adapted front-end loader, they are brought in by train and truck.

The yellow room picks up where the editorial tour left off. In this room, the laid out pages are turned into negatives. The negatives, similar in principle to color film, are the actual size of a newspaper page. Once the negatives are made, they are transferred onto an aluminum plate using a special light comparable to sunlight that etches the metal. The plates are actually affixed to the presses to make the newspapers.

The presses provide an interesting look to the newspaper. You will be able to walk through a press station and see how the plates fit on the press and where the newsprint feeds through the press. The production facility has six presses, even though they are all connected and look like one big machine. In the middle of the presses the workers interface with computers. Here they are able to program the presses for ink color and quantity. Pressmen do much more than just watch the machines run. They are constantly busy pulling out samples to check ink and color registration on the tables next to the press. Here they compare the original ink color with the samples pulled and make any needed adjustments using computers.

The papers, once off the presses, are grabbed by a hook and fed to the holding and insertion part of the building. Here different sections are stacked, ready to be collated and sent to their final destination. Advertisements, comics, and different sections of the newspaper on pallets are readied for the insertion machine.

SAN ANTONIO WINERY

The last place you'd expect to find a winery is downtown Los Angeles, but that is one of the surprises of the San Antonio Winery. Located a mile from City Hall, wine connoisseurs know this older winery produces great quality close to home. In the early 1900's there were more than 100 producing wineries in the Los Angeles basin. Today, this winery is the only one still at its original location. Recognized as an important part of Los Angeles history, the City of Los Angeles established it as a cultural and historical landmark.

The opportunity to learn more about the wine production process actually starts in the parking lot where a wine press and storage bin from the early 1900's are on display. Inside, the personal touch of the winery can be seen immediately. This family business has been handcrafting wine for four generations.

The tour at the winery lasts around 30 minutes and gives an up close and personal view of the vintner process. Leading the tour, the vintner or one of his associates will detail the traditional process of winemaking. Once the grapes have been processed, visitors will see barrels where the wine is stored. After viewing the packaging process visitors are taken to the sampling room for a tasting.

WELLS FARGO HISTORY MUSEUM

Long before there was a U.S. Postal Service or FedEx, there was Wells Fargo. The preserved stagecoaches that carried most of the mail, commodities and passengers across the early United States can be seen at the Wells Fargo History Museum. Located across the pedestrian way of the Wells Fargo Bank in downtown Los Angeles, this breeze into the past is a great opportunity to see how the West and the State of California were settled.

TAKE THE TOUR

WHERE TO GO
333 South Grand
Los Angeles, CA 90071

WHEN TO GO
Self-Guided Tour
Monday - Friday 9am - 5pm

DEGREE OF DIFFICULTY
Easy

CONTACT
213.253.7166
www.wellsfargo.com

Just inside the museum, a restored mail facility creates the scene. Neatly put together, visitors get the chance to see how the office of the local Wells Fargo looked. Busy with paperwork, mail and people, the office was responsible for the correspondence of the area. As technology developed, the telegraph was also found at this office.

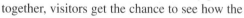

It is interesting to note that the stagecoach located in the front of the building has not been restored. The wear of the seats and the wood brings to life the reality of the west. Just next to the coach are the coach boxes. Passengers would pack their belongings into these small containers, taking next to nothing on their journey. Other boxes would carry mail, gold, documents, and supplies needed on the way. Near the back of the building, there is a stagecoach visitors can climb into for a photo opportunity.

There is an excellent display of artifacts from the Old West. Relics, such as an ore cart, along with an axe and pick from the California Gold Rush are on display. Gold pans once used by prospectors hoping to strike it rich can be found along the walls. The Gold Rush, which helped develop California, was also responsible for making Wells Fargo successful. Today, the focus of Wells Fargo is no longer mail, but banking.

Wells Fargo is a leading national bank respectfully known all over the United States.

Tours FOR **FREE**™

FREDERICK'S OF HOLLYWOOD
LINGERIE MUSEUM

GORDON HOWARD
MUSEUM COMPLEX

GUIDE DOGS OF AMERICA

HOLLYWOOD WALK OF STARS

KRISPY KREME DONUTS

ORCUTT RANCH
HORTICULTURE CENTER

THE NETHERCUTT COLLECTION

THE NETHERCUTT MUSEUM

THE ROAD TO HOLLYWOOD

WILLIAM S. HART MUSEUM

HOLLYWOOD

& SAN FERNANDO VALLEY

FREDERICK'S OF HOLLYWOOD LINGERIE MUSEUM

TAKE THE TOUR

WHERE TO GO
6608 Hollywood Blvd
Hollywood, CA 90028

WHEN TO GO
Self-Guided Tour
Monday - Friday
10am - 9pm
Saturday 10am -7pm
Sunday 1am - 6pm

DEGREE OF DIFFICULTY
Easy

CONTACT
323.466.8506

Anyone looking for something silly to do should check out the store just below the Frederick's of Hollywood Corporate Offices on Hollywood Boulevard. Developing museum to honor some of the most covered garments his is a tour that is definitely worth a peek.

What is underwear without Madonna? That question vas what Frederick's of Hollywood must have been thinking when they put together this museum. On display re items from Madonna's private collection (even if she lid wear it on stage). Visitors can also see Tom Hanks' boxer shorts from the film Forest Gump. Not to be left out, several stars have donated some of their intimate clothing to the Frederick's of Hollywood museum, all of which is dutifully on display.

Much of the lingerie on exhibit is tastefully placed on manikins to demonstrate how they were worn. Down the hallway from the museum, visitors can follow the evolution of panties and bras over the decades. From exotic to common, this is the place to see it all. Toward the end the museum is a unique look at sizes and shapes of people and how they fit into their underwear.

Celebrity Lingerie
Now Showing

Madonna	Cybill Shepherd
Elizabeth Taylor	Tom Hanks
Milton Berle	Joan Collins
Rosie O'Donnell	Lana Turner
Cher	Ava Gardner

TAKE THE TOUR

WHERE TO GO
1015 W. Olive
Burbank, CA 91506

WHEN TO GO
Self-Guided Tours
Guided Tours
Sunday 12noon – 4pm
Reservations Required

DEGREE OF DIFFICULTY
Easy

CONTACT
818.841.6333

GORDON R. HOWARD MUSEUM

The city of Burbank has more television studios than any city in California. The tour of the Gordon R. Howard Museum focuses on the role these studios play in the entertainment industry as well as the history of the city. Before the growth of the television industry and the accompanying studios, Burbank was best known for the airplanes built at the Lockheed Aircraft plant. That factory has since relocated, but the entertainment industry has more than replaced the 94,000 who worked there building airplanes.

The tour of the museum gives visitors a fun journey back to the early days of Burbank and television, beginning with Dr. David Burbank who owned much of the property that is now the city of Burbank. A dentist, Dr. Burbank owned a sheep ranch and worked in the community until the drought of 1886 forced him to sell out. The museum has several relics from this era, from horse-drawn buggies to period clothes.

The City of Burbank has grown over time and flourished during World War II when the Lockheed plant built planes for the war. An entire display covers the Lockheed aircraft production. Several different types of aircraft were produced in Burbank and small models of these are on display.

Today, Burbank is known for the influence it has on studios in California. Nickelodeon, NBC and Disney are a few of the major studios that flourish in the area. The museum put together an entire display about the beginning of broadcasting where visitors can see how the studios were set up. For those who enjoy antique automobiles, a stop in the main area of the museum is essential to see the classic cars and trucks on display.

Using interactive elements, the museum has a section where visitors can look into windows and listen to what is going on with old-fashioned telephone cups. This is exciting for kids. After touring the main museum, visitors can walk through the gate and look at the old fashioned house that is on Olive Street, or check out the aircraft on display right next door. Both are great places to take a snapshot or two.

GUIDE DOGS OF AMERICA

The Guide Dogs of America is an organization that helps visually impaired individuals become more independent with the use of trained dogs. The organization is supported solely from donations and volunteers. The guide dog training process takes an immense amount of work, but as will be seen on this tour, these dogs, the staff and the volunteers stay focused and work hard. The training and selection process for the dogs is intense, only 40 percent of puppies that begin the program will become guide dogs. The rest are disqualified for not responding to training or for health reasons.

TAKE THE TOUR

WHERE TO GO
13445 Glenoaks Boulevard
Sylmar, CA 91342

WHEN TO GO
Guided Tours
Reservations Required

DEGREE OF DIFFICULTY
Easy

CONTACT
818.362.5834
www.guidedogsofamerica.org

The dogs used in this program are mostly bred at the facility. Each litter of puppies is assigned a letter of the alphabet and all the puppies' names start with that letter. Once the animals are old enough they are placed with volunteers. The new homes in which they are placed helps desensitize the dogs to sights and sounds. For 16 months the dogs live and grow with the volunteers. Once they are old enough, the dog returns to the facility and begins the next stage of their working life. For six weeks the dogs are worked daily, trained to understand commands and becoming familiar with new surroundings. After the commands are learned, their final training is next. The dog must learn to disobey if there is possible danger. This command is used if there is oncoming traffic and one needs to cross the street.

After the dog is ready to be placed with an individual, the next step is connecting the dog with the owner. People from all over the United States come to the facility in Sylmar and stay for four weeks. This allows the dog and owner to become familiar with each other. The process of the team working is emphasized as the two begin a new life together.

This tour gives visitors a chance to see the dormitories where the dogs and people are matched, the training grounds and a wonderful selection of photographs displaying the guide dogs. Bringing together a dog and a person in need, this organization finds joy in helping others.

HOLLYWOOD WALK OF STARS

Being star struck isn't difficult on this tour. Bring a camera and start a journey of the entertainment industry along the Walk of Stars. Covering more than 10 blocks, visitors have the chance to walk along, enjoying the California sun, taking stock of the famous stars of yesterday and today.

It is best to start the tours at the legendary Mann's Chinese Theater. Begin in the courtyard where visitors can compare footprints with stars that left imprints of their hands and feet. Right in front, Roy Rogers and Mickey Rooney left their impression in cement.

Walking along Hollywood Boulevard, the stars are found honoring all types of famous people. Honoring performers of all stripes - from actors to musicians to directors - by placing a bronze plaque with a star on it in the sidewalk is unique to Hollywood. The stars - actual tiles of bronze with a star's name and type of performer - are spaced about 10 feet apart along this walk.

On a nice day, visitors can take time enjoying the different tiles and people watching. From the tourists to the eccentric, the people who walk along Hollywood Boulevard are entertaining all by themselves.

TAKE THE TOUR

WHERE TO GO
Hollywood and Vine Streets
Hollywood, CA 90028

WHEN TO GO
Self-Guided Tour
Daily

DEGREE OF DIFFICULTY
Moderate

CONTACT
323.469.8311
www.hollywoodcoc.org

KRISPY KREME DONUTS

TAKE THE TOUR

WHERE TO GO
7249 Van Nuys Blvd.
Van Nuys, CA 91405

WHEN TO GO
Self-Guided Tours
5:30 - 11am Daily

DEGREE OF DIFFICULTY
Easy

CONTACT
818.908.9113
www.krispykreme.com

For everyone who likes a good, hot pastry, Krispy Kreme is the place to tour. Hundreds of donuts roll off the production line hourly at this location. The favorite donut at Kristy Kreme has to be the glazed donut. Take an extra minute and instead of using the drive thru, check out the donut making process through the observation window inside.

Krispy Kreme welcomes the prospect of showing the process of making donuts to the entire community. The windows are right next to machines making donuts so visitors can watch employees in action. Early in the morning, school kids can be found watching intently through the window, hoping to pick their next donut.

The donut batter, shaped in traditional size is placed on trays toward the far end of the machine. Once the donuts are cooked, they are fried in a tub of heated grease. Hot and floating, the donut cooks while slowly moving along, eventually turned by one of the bakers to cook both sides evenly. Once the cooking is finished, the glaze is next. Moving on a slotted belt, the donuts are showered under a coat of glaze. As they move through, the glaze drips off and runs into a tightly sealed capturing container. The belt then pushes the donut along two to four feet until it is ready to eat.

ORCUTT RANCH
HORTICULTURE CENTER

TAKE THE TOUR

WHERE TO GO
23600 Roscoe Blvd
West Hills, CA 91304

WHEN TO GO
Self Guided Tours
8am - 5pm Daily

DEGREE OF DIFFICULTY
Easy

CONTACT
818.346.7449

The tour of the Orcutt Ranch lets visitors experience a graceful and secluded garden paradise. Nestled in the foothills of west San Fernando Valley, the property was the vacation residence of William and Mary Orcutt. William was in the first graduating class of Stanford University and became Vice President of Union Oil. His wife, Mary, was active in the community and served as an Olympic hostess in 1932, the highlight of which was a gala reception in the gardens.

The estate was originally known as Rancho Sombre del Roble or "ranch shaded by the oak," which is only steps away from the door of the ranch. The planning of the ranch began in 1929 with the original home, which comprised 3,060 square feet of floor space and surrounding grounds of more than 200 acres. The lush property was planted with a variety of fruit and nut trees, including grapefruit, oranges and walnuts throughout the rolling hills. Flowers bloom all year long on the ranch and at one time more than 500 rose bushes were counted in the garden.

Among the trees, citrus groves and flowers are stone statues, brick walkways, benches and stone walls. A group of three muses carved from Italian marble overlook the rose garden. The opportunity to walk around after the tour is always available. It is a great place to bring a lunch and enjoy the day.

The Los Angeles City Recreation and Parks Department purchased the ranch in 1966. The tour offers a chance to explore this oasis located only minutes from the city.

THE NETHERCUTT COLLECTION

Across the street from the Nethercutt Museum of 100 vintage automobiles is the private collection of the Nethercutt family, which can only be seen by appointment. The collection includes more automobiles, musical instruments and more. The residence displays items that are in working condition, giving visitors an opportunity to step back in time and relive the domestic life of yesterday. Because this tour is quite popular, plan to make reservations three to six weeks in advance. Do not forget that there is a dress code. Blue jeans, shorts and t-shirts are not allowed and the guides prefer that visitors dress up to attend the tour.

The tour is divided up into several sections, appealing to different parts of the group.

Among the items on display are classic automobiles, musical instruments, antique glass, and one of the largest automobile hood ornament collections anywhere. Taking in a bit of all of the different collections, guests can plan on being on tour for a solid three hours and, depending on the pace of the group, it could be longer. Make sure to wear comfortable shoes as there is extended standing. There are chairs on the different floors, so there are opportunities to rest.

The tour starts on the first floor. Stepping into a showroom made especially for the Nethercutt Collection, visitors are exposed to a dozen vintage automobiles. The guide explains the importance of these autos by describing where they came from and the condition of each before restoration. Up the grand stairway, live recordings are played on the player grand piano. Different than live performances, the mechanical piano actually works by following a series of punched holes on a roll of paper. This process reproduces the live performance exactly as played.

Passing the piano, the tour continues into the glass collection. From flowers to china, the art in this room is quite splendid. The famous hood ornament collection is toward the end of the room. This is the largest collection of hood ornaments known to man, ranging from glass to metal in all sorts of designs and automobile mascots.

On the next floor visitors are privileged to hear some of the music machines created during the 1800 and 1900's. Gigantic machines found in saloons and outdoor carousels line the walls. After an explanation of the history and function, some of the machines are played for visitors. This music doesn't sound like something on the radio, it is a mixing melody from the different instruments mechanically played from behind the wooden boards. The music created is simple. Every machine sounds unusual with the most interesting saved for last.

In the middle of the room a gigantic organ with four rows of keys to play and too many foot peddles to keep straight. This organ is one of the largest pipe organs in the country. The melody played from the organ is quite spectacular, but so is the view behind the windows shades. Pipes of every shape and size howl when they are played. Playing several songs, the organ is the highlight of the tour.

The guide on this tour goes into details about the different pieces displayed on all three floors. Visitors are sure to walk away surprised at the experience of such an immense collection.

TAKE THE TOUR

WHERE TO GO
15200 Bledsoe Street
Sylmar, CA 91342

WHEN TO GO
Guided Tours
Reservations Required

DEGREE OF DIFFICULTY
Moderate

CONTACT
818.367.2251
www.nethercuttcollection.org

THE NETHERCUTT MUSEUM

The Nethercutt Museum is one of the secret treasures of Southern California. Not to be confused with the Nethercutt Collection across the street, this collection is focused solely on rare vehicles. Highlighting the working models of automobiles from yesteryear, this is a great opportunity to see antique cars in excellent condition.

The Nethercutt's have collected workable art over the years. Finding beauty in functional items, their collection grew over time to an enormous assortment of cars. Becoming bigger and bigger, the collection blossomed into a museum that opened its doors to the public in 2000. More than 100 specialty automobiles are on display. Completely restored and in fine working condition, the cars could easily be driven off the showroom and onto the street for a Sunday drive.

The actual museum could almost be described as a new car showroom. The collection includes Packard, Duesenberg, Pierce-Arrow, and Rolls-Royce as well as many other automobile models. Lined up along the walls and down the middle of the room, the collection travels back in time to see how different automobiles were built compared to the cars today. The order in which the automobiles are lined up gives visitors the chance to actually see the historical and engineering changes over time. New designs, more gadgets and more room and comfort are a few of the main changes. Giving you the most for your looking pleasure, each car has an information card in front describing the make and model of the car. Also the card gives the retail value when the car was originally purchased.

In keeping with the classic ambience, the owner of the collection asks that visitors adhere to a dress code by wearing appropriate clothes during the visit. This means no blue jeans, shorts or t-shirts. The other important rule is, unlike the showroom at your local car dealership, touching is not allowed.

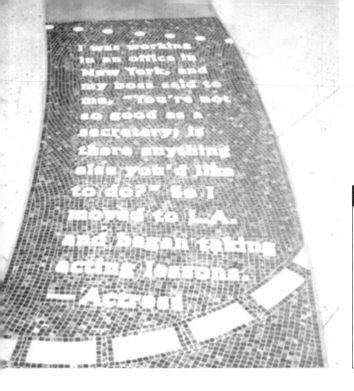

ROAD TO HOLLYWOOD

Anyone who has ever dreamed of becoming a movie star should visit The Road to Hollywood. Located at the Hollywood and Highland Mall, this tour is one not to be missed.

The movie business is tough to get into, so the mall set up a walking tour that shows visitors how several movie business professionals paid their dues to make it in Hollywood. Starting at the street, there are rectangle tiles that guide you along the journey. Placing an emphasis on those who made it into the business the hard way, visitors get can read quotes and realize all the hurdles they had to clear on the way.

Taken from directors, movie stars and others, the anonymous quotes lay bare the business of show business and shows just how hard it is to become a star. As you wind around, you learn more and more about the struggle of those people involved in movies and television.

The end of the tour offers a real treat. As with many who have come to Hollywood, visitors will get to see how they became a movie star in a 45-minute walk. Creating a picture perfect setting, visitors will get to take a few snapshots on the couch with the Hollywood sign in the background.

This is a great opportunity to learn more about the movie business. People who write, produce and make movies are hard working individuals, and this tour offers a glimpse of what it takes to succeed in Hollywood.

WILLIAM S. HART MUSEUM

Los Angeles has always been known for its ties to the movie industry and the William S. Hart Museum is one of the best places to explore the history of movies and the people in them. In the beginning, motion pictures were silent movies. Audiences would be entertained with a screen of action and the dialog of the stars read between the scenes. Accompanied by live music, going to the picture show was a totally different experience than today's theaters with soundtracks that make the seats rumble.

William Hart was a big name in the silent movie industry. Better known as Two Guns Bill, he created the good guy image that is still found today in the movie business. His success as a star in 69 Westerns lasted more than 10 years before he retired in 1925. His last film, and probably the most successful, was Tumbleweeds.

The tour at the museum is a chance to examine the life of this early film star. As is fitting with a grand home, the mansion is on top of a hill, making it a bit of a walk from the parking lot. The entire house has 20 rooms, seven bathrooms and sweeping views in every direction.

Being that the whole home is open, visitors get the chance to see his entire Western art collection, which includes several pieces of Navajo art he received as gifts. The tour starts in the big room on the first floor. Here Mr. Hart entertained his guests at lavish parties that set the standard for what is now known as the Hollywood lifestyle. The mansion has many modern elements not usually found in a home of the 1920's. A good example of this is next to the elaborate dining room table there is a warmer above the stove. While eating dinner, the pans could be set upon the grill to keep the food warm.

Upstairs, visitors will find the living room displaying where Hart was at home. Here an early version of the home theater can be found. The room can be transformed into a theater with the projection booth behind the wall. Upstairs, a telephone booth - similar to one you would find on the street - is built into the wall.

Mr. Hart loved dogs and the bedrooms on the tour are proof of this. His original bedroom was transformed into his dogs' bedroom when his two large harlequin Great Danes became too big to sleep with him. Instead of throwing them off the bed, he decided to let them keep the room for themselves and he built another bedroom. The dog beds for both dogs are on display as well as their collars.

Directly below the Hart Museum, visitors will find a farm with animals and a relaxing atmosphere. In the spirit of the Wild West, a small herd of buffalo can be observed from the hillside.

Also in this area, the bunkhouse at the base of the hill is open for public viewing. Seven fully decorated rooms are on display to show how people lived in the old West. Pictures of Mr. Hart and relics from the past can be seen through the plastic windows on this small self-guided tour.

UCLA CAMPUS

TAKE THE TOUR

WHERE TO GO
405 Hilgard Avenue
Los Angeles, CA 90095

WHEN TO GO
Self-Guided
Guide available on website
Guided
Reservations Required

DEGREE OF DIFFICULTY:
Moderate

CONTACT
(310) 825-4321
www.ucla.edu

The Bears are known to call the University of California Los Angeles home. Mascot of sporting events for the university and found walking on campus close to the student center (a metal replica of course) the tour gives visitors a chance to find out why these bears call UCLA home.

The tour, for college freshman and anyone interested in finding out more about the university, is approximately two hours long. Current students give the tours that cover the historical and contemporary issues of the school. You will find yourself swept back in time learning information about the school while visiting the grounds of a busy place.

On August 29, 1882, the Los Angeles Branch of the State Normal School was opened. Just a simple teaching college at the time, the original site of the school is the now present Los Angeles Central Library. Moving with the times, the school added science and letters of instruction. The school was moved to Hollywood after the City of Los Angeles grew to 350,000 people and the attendance of the school outgrew that location. Becoming a four year institution, the university continued to soar with the population.

A permanent site for the university was not finalized until September 27, 1927. Acknowledging the west was growing a decision was made to use 400 acres in Westwood. Royce Hall, Powell Library, Haines and Kinsey Halls are original buildings formed in the middle of the land.

Today the campus has over 419 acres with 163 buildings. Luckily you don't have to see all the buildings, but your tour will cover the main campus and buildings of major interest. You also will get the chance to see many of the 36,900 students who are enrolled in various academic programs.

Tours *FOR* FREE™

**BUNGALOW HEAVEN
LANDMARK TOUR**

**JET PROPULSION
LABORATORY**

THE OLD MILL

PASADENA

& SURROUNDING AREA

BUNGALOW HEAVEN LANDMARK TOUR

TAKE THE TOUR

WHERE TO GO
Pasadena Visitors &
Convention Bureau
171 South Los Robles Ave.
Pasadena, CA 91101

WHEN TO GO
Self Guided Tours
Monday - Friday 8am - 5pm
Saturday 10am - 4pm

DEGREE OF DIFFICULTY
Easy

CONTACT
626.795.9311
www.pasadenacal.com

Located in the heart of Pasadena, the Bungalow tour is a unique opportunity to step back into a lifestyle of the past. Homes known as bungalows were popular in this area because they were functional, practical and easily built - a must due to the tremendous growth at the time. Bungalows saw their heyday between 1900 and 1920, at the height of the Arts and Crafts movement. Combining Asian, European and American influences, bungalows sought to combine harmony of design and function, coupled with quality construction and simplicity.

The tour begins at the Pasadena Visitors Bureau to obtain an easy-to-follow map. Driving down North Mar Vista, the 1910 bungalow built by contractor Henry McKeen is first on the list. Further down the way is a bungalow that belonged to the Nobel Prize winner Linus Pauling. Bungalows were often designed to be expanded as the family grew. Some of the houses on these blocks have been expanded to include new rooms or entire second floors. On East Claremont, there is a small, stucco 'storybook' bungalow designed and built by E.A. Daniell. It is worth stopping to admire the workmanship and attention to detail, not to mention the fine woodwork.

The self-guided Bungalow Heaven Landmark Tour includes roughly 12 blocks of houses, and walk the tour on a nice day.

JET PROPULSION LABORATORY

It is hard to imagine a small remote controlled vehicle exploring the surface of a planet more than 54 million miles away. But that is just what NASA did with the Mars Rover, built in Pasadena. The tour of the Jet Propulsion Lab offers a look into how NASA builds satellites, communicates with them and uses data from those satellites to conduct various experiments.

The tour starts with a 20 minute presentation on the 20-year history of the Jet Propulsion Laboratory. The auditorium contains full-size replicas of several satellites built by the lab and now orbiting the earth. After the presentation, visitors can explore the museum where more replicas of satellites and several interactive exhibits bring the earlier presentation to life. Of special note is the prototype of the Mars Rover.

After a walk across the campus, visitors are lead to the command station where orbiting satellites are controlled. Hundreds of miles above the earth, these satellites are constantly collecting, transmitting and receiving data from the command center where each is carefully tracked and monitored. Among the data being collected are measurements of various physical features and geological trends on the earth's surface. Some interplanetary satellites take six to 12 hours to transmit data because they are so far away. Huge window panels provide a view of the vast computer network needed for this intensive process. On the far side of the room, visitors get the chance to see a scale representation of the solar system. The guide talks about the planets and how they are unique and explains the procedures that take place here, making this room so important to scientists.

The final stop on the tour is the production laboratories. Scientists and engineers

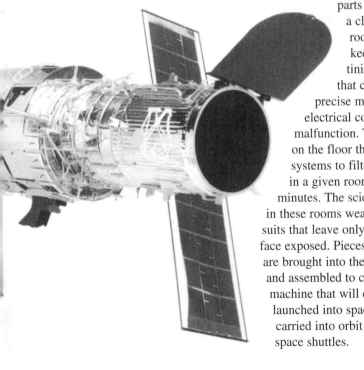

assemble the different parts of a satellite in a clean room. These rooms are sealed to keep out even the tiniest speck of dust that could cause the precise mechanical and electrical components to malfunction. There are grates on the floor that enable special systems to filter all of the air in a given room every 10 minutes. The scientists who work in these rooms wear dust-proof suits that leave only their hands and face exposed. Pieces of the satellites are brought into the room, tested and assembled to create the final machine that will eventually be launched into space on a rocket or carried into orbit on one of the space shuttles.

THE OLD MILL

Roughly two miles away from the Mission San Gabriel, the two-story Old Mill stands as a reminder of the importance grinding grain had in providing food. The Mission is the fourth of California's 21 Missions and was established by the Spanish Franciscan Order in 1771. On a hillside in San Marino, the building is operated by The Old Mill Foundation.

Completed in 1816, the two-story structure was made with the best materials available at the time. The lower walls are five feet think and made from oven baked brick and volcanic tuff. Upstairs, the walls are built of layers of sun-dried adobe slabs. The entire outside walls were then covered with a mortar made from lime derived from burnt seashells.

The gardens that surround the mill are a fine place to sit and relax. Plants in full bloom escort you as you weave around the garden pathway. Originally comprising more than 500 acres including the garden, vineyard and orchard, the mill complex was part of State Assemblyman Col. E.J.C. Kerwen's residence starting in 1858. A large open patio behind the mill was a popular location for festivals and celebrations of the day. Today the garden area is much smaller, but no less enjoyable, and a great place to bring a lunch to eat under the gazebo after your tour.

TAKE THE TOUR

WHERE TO GO
1120 Old Mill Road
San Marino, CA 91108

WHEN TO GO
Self-Guided Tours
Tuesday - Sunday 1-4pm

DEGREE OF DIFFICULTY
Moderate

CONTACT
626.449.5458

The tour begins in the grinding room of the mill. Grain harvested on mission lands was ground between the heavy millstones. The bottom stone remained stationary while a waterwheel turned the top stone. Though nothing remains of the original waterwheels, a set of millstones was discovered by General George Patton and are preserved on the patio.

The upper room is where the milled grain was stored and downstairs, in the wheel chamber, visitors can see the low-vaulted ceiling, a traditional element in mission architecture. On display in this room is a working model of the grist mill as it looked in 1816.

Tours FOR **FREE**™

BANNING RESIDENCE MUSEUM

BELL OF FRIENDSHIP

CABRILLO MARINE AQUARIUM

CASA DE TORTUGA

CRYSTAL CATHEDRAL

DRUM BARRACKS
CIVIL WAR MUSEUM

GETTY CENTER

LONG BEACH AIRPORT

LOS ANGELES MARITIME
MUSEUM

LOS ANGELES TEMPLE

LUMMIS HOUSE

MARINE MAMMAL CARE
CENTER AT FORT MACARTHUR

RANCHO LOS ALAMITOS

WAYFARERS CHAPEL

LA COAST

BANNING
RESIDENCE MUSEUM

TAKE THE TOUR

WHERE TO GO
401 East M Street
Wilmington, CA 90748

WHEN TO GO
Guided Tours
Tuesday, Wednesday,
Thursday 12:30pm, 1:30pm,
2:30pm
Saturday, Sunday
12:30pm, 1:30pm, 2:30pm,
3:30pm

DEGREE OF DIFFICULTY
Moderate

CONTACT
310.548.7777
www.banningmuseum.org

The Banning Residence Museum offers an opportunity o explore the forefathers and the establishment of Los Angeles. Visitors will be amazed at how one man's dedication and strong will brought the community ogether. This tour offers an opportunity to understand vhy Los Angeles was built the way it was and how it became modern city of the 21st century.

In 1851, Phineas Banning arrived in Los Angeles, the year after California became a state. Like many others, he ame to California to start anew. The life he created as a rancher wasn't bad, but Banning saw an opportunity to better the community and dreamed of building a tandard port for ships to import and export goods. Known today as the Port of Los Angeles, it is still in use today and is one of the largest ports on the West Coast. Other significant contributions of Banning include the Civil War compound. With he land he donated to the North, troops trained for the war effort to travel East rom California.

The historical significance of the Banning House can't be seen from the outside, but visitors can see the beauty of this Greek Revival residence. Three stories high, he walk-in basement can be accessed from the East side of the house. This is where parties took place as members of the community came to feast and dance. Large trees surrounding the house give it a certain calmness and Southern charm. Behind the house are some of the original barns.

The tour of this 23-room house begins in the basement with photographs of the family. From there the actual tour of the house begins in the parlor inside the front door as the docent guides describe the different social events that took place in the room. The details of the room are also shared with guests to better understand why certain types of furniture were purchased by the Banning family. The tour continues through the first floor where visitors will see Phineas' office. Notice the record books as well as the day-to-day items he used. The preservation of artifacts is amazing as most of the displayed items are original Banning documents.

The kitchen, the library and the hallway are grand. Upstairs several bedrooms that overlook the park are available for viewing as well. One striking thing about the bedrooms is the armories. The tax structure of the times was a major concern for ranchers in the region. So to avoid being taxed for every room, closets were not built. Instead beautiful stand-alone cabinets with doors were used for storing everything from dishes to clothing.

The Banning Residence Museum is more than just a museum to browse. Bringing the innovation and surroundings of a key man who helped develop Los Angeles, visitors leave appreciating how one man could be so important to an entire community. The house itself is a mansion even today's standards.

BELL OF FRIENDSHIP

TAKE THE TOUR

WHERE TO GO
S. Gaffey St. @ W 37th St.
Angels Gate Park
San Pedro, CA 90731

WHEN TO GO
Self Guided Tour
7am to 6pm daily

DEGREE OF DIFFICULTY
Easy

CONTACT
310.548.7705

Driving up to Angel Park is a beautiful way to spend the afternoon. Looking out over the rippling waves of the ocean and seeing the boat traffic coming and going through the Port of Los Angeles, no matter what the weather, there is no place better to stop than at the Bell of Friendship.

The bell is easily seen from the parking lot overlooking the ocean under a brightly painted pagoda-style belfry. The tour begins across the parking lot. The information Center for the Korean Bell of Friendship is open daily, sharing information about the culture of America and Korea. The walls are full of photographs and commentary giving a historic look into Korea and some of their people who have come to America. The exhibits give an idea of the struggles in the past and the culture. On the table inside the door, visitors will have the opportunity to pick up more information about Korea and a Korean map.

Next up is looking at the actual Friendship Bell. Several strange stick creatures next to the sidewalk leading up to the bell are worth a look. The bell is the same size as the largest bronze bell in existence in East Asia. Eight feet high, it is beautifully placed underneath the belfry along with the log bell striker. The engravings on the sides of the bell include images of the Statue of Liberty and a Korean Spirit holding Korea's national flower, the Rose of Sharon. Given to the United States on July 4th, 1976, the Korean Government hoped to foster unity between the two countries.

It took more than 20 skilled craftsmen six months to complete the molding of the bell. The bell is mostly an alloy of copper and tin with hints of gold, silver, nickel and other materials to give it the perfect ring. The bell is only struck four times a year including July 4th and New Year's Day, it rings for five minutes, giving off a rumbling sound that fills Angel Park. The Bell of Friendship is a great cultural resource that focuses on the possibility of two countries, no matter how ethnically different, striving to live and work together for the unified goal of peace and friendship.

CABRILLO MARINE AQUARIUM

TAKE THE TOUR

WHERE TO GO
3720 Stephen White Drive
San Pedro, CA 90731

WHEN TO GO
Self-Guided Tours
Tuesday – Friday
12 noon to 5pm
Saturday - Sunday
10am to 5 p.m.

DEGREE OF DIFFICULTY
Easy

CONTACT
310.548.7562
www.cabrilloaq.org

For visitors looking for a whale of a time, the Cabrillo Marine Aquarium is the place to go. Located in the beautiful city of San Pedro, the aquarium is an active research facility open to the public. Since it is a research facility, visitors are not going to find a fancy finish on the walls like the aquarium across the bay. The beauty of the facility is the focus on learning about the ocean and the creatures that live in it.

Located on Cabrillo Beach, visitors will know they have found the right place when they see the blue sperm whale in the parking lot. To give an idea of how big these creatures are, the blue outline of a whale was made on the wall of the main building. The overwhelming size of this creature gives some thought to what could fit inside a whale.

Inside visitors get to see the actual creatures that roam the ocean. Starting with how fish and mammals survive in the ocean, an interesting exhibit of the surf and the motion of the waves take this journey underwater. The sand, plants and fish move with the water creating continuous motion. Other exhibits include sponges, legged creatures and, of course, fish. Jellyfish, lobsters, and even shrimp are on display in tanks among the dark halls.

Behind the aquarium, during special hours, a tide pool is open for kids. Using two fingers, they can feel sponges, starfish and even a stingray. An employee of the aquarium is on hand to answer questions while keeping an eye on the tank to make sure the animals are happy.

For those who find sea lions, seals, dolphins, whales and other sea mammals interesting, don't forget to check out the last part of the aquarium. Focusing on the other animals that live in the water, the aquarium has different bones on display giving visitors the chance to see how big these animals are. Another interesting aspect of this section is the birds overhead. A large stuffed pelican is flying above with his wings spread wide.

The last part of the tour is a walk through the whale graveyard. Here is the chance to take a few photos. Bones from the larger mammals stick out of the ground to give visitors an idea of the enormous size of these mammals.

CASA DE TORTUGA

TAKE THE TOUR

WHERE TO GO
10455 Circulo de Zapata
Fountain Valley, CA 92708

WHEN TO GO
Guided Tours
Reservations Required

DEGREE OF DIFFICULTY
Easy

CONTACT
714.962.0612

For those who like turtles or tortoises, this free tour is not to be missed. The collection at Casa de Tortuga includes over 800 animals in a 7,500 square foot complex. Mr. Walter Allen, the owner of Casa de Tortuga, along with the other animal caretakers provides daily food, water and nutrients for the animals. This popular tour tends to fill up fast so it is important to call ahead for reservations.

Before starting the tour, the guide will review a few basic rules. The most important rule is to stay on the rocks. Since there are animals everywhere, stepping in the wrong place would definitely not be a pretty sight. Another rule is to keep with the group. With the animal's safety in mind, these are pretty easy rules to follow.

There are over 100 different types of turtles at the Casa. The beginning of the tour will highlight a few basic kinds, including the California Turtle. Around the side of the building the most basic of turtles, the red neck sliders, can be found munching on lettuce. Having their own pond, these smart long neck-turtles like the attention they get when the group stops to admire them. Further back in the complex roam the gigantic tortoises. These impressive animals weigh up to 800 pounds with a shell the size of a chair. In this small area there are seven different varieties of turtles and tortoises all beautiful examples of their species.

While Casa de Tortuga seems small, around each corner there are more animals and interesting displays. Around the corner from the gigantic tortoises is a 5,000 gallon outdoor water pond that is home to over 100 turtles. Floating around as well as sunning next to the plants, there is an amazing harmony between the different species.

The tour returns the same way that it entered the complex giving the opportunity to see things that might have been missed the first time or to catch a few snapshots. The final stop on the tour will be the glass windows on the back of the building. Here are different aquariums displaying rare and unusual turtles. From the alligator turtle to the Indonesia turtle, visitors get an up-close look at the varied characteristics of the turtles. The kitchen, close to the turtle display looks like a regular kitchen except that it is for preparing turtle food. Each room in the house focuses on different needs for the caring of turtles and tortoises.

Although Casa de Tortuga is in a residential area, no one lives at the house. According to the guide it is exclusively a turtle dwelling.

CRYSTAL CATHEDRAL

TAKE THE TOUR

WHERE TO GO
12141 Lewis Street
Garden Grove, CA 92840

WHEN TO GO
Guided Tours
Monday – Saturday
9am - 3:30pm

DEGREE OF DIFFICULTY
Easy

CONTACT
714.971.4013
www.crystalcathedral.org

Those traveling on I-5 can easily see the Crystal Cathedral and the temple glistening in the sun. The guided tour includes details about the Crystal Cathedral, the gardens and grounds and information about the ministry.

Known for the weekly broadcasts of Robert Schuller's Hour of Power, the grounds reflect the preacher's focus on the bible using the artistic medium of bronze. The life size sculptures found in and around the Cathedral detail scenes from various biblical stories. A particularly interesting piece is the one directly in front of the church. Focusing on the journey of Jesus as a child, he and his mother, Mary are riding on a donkey as his father Joseph is walking along side. To help humanize the events depicted, the statues are actually painted to bring out lifelike details.

The tour also gives some background of the church and the ministry. Taking visitors around the gardens, the experienced guides explain the different sculptures and the stories behind them.

Referencing the bible, this is an opportunity to see how the stories unfold in the eyes of the artists.

Touring the inside the church, visitors quickly realize how much larger the cathedral is than it appears to be on the television program. Housing one of the largest pip organs in the country, the music in the church vibrates off the glass walls. Completely surrounded in glass, the primary light in the church is from the sun. Taking a minute to look up, one can see the continuous patters of different shapes created by the housings that hold the glass. These housings form triangles upon squares to create a beautiful patter that captures the eye and the imagination. Just the experience of standing in such a majestic work of art makes this tour worth the trip.

TAKE THE TOUR

WHERE TO GO
1052 Banning Boulevard
Wilmington, CA 90744

WHEN TO GO
Guided Tours
Tuesday, Wednesday,
Thursday
on the hour from
10am to 1pm
Saturday and Sunday
on the half hour from
11:30 a.m. to 2:30 p.m.

DEGREE OF DIFFICULTY
Moderate

CONTACT
310.548.7509
www.drumbarracks.org

DRUM BARRACKS CIVIL WAR MUSEUM

Most people do not realize the role California played in the Civil War. The tour at the Drum Barracks Civil War Museum is a great opportunity to learn more about how this turbulent time in American history reached clear across the west to Wilmington. From 1861 to 1865 about 17,000 Californians served in The Civil War. The guided tour will open visitor's eyes on how much Californians were involved despite their geographic location.

The military base was given by Phineas Banning and B.D. Wilson who lived less than a mile away. Around sixty acres of land was sold to the U.S. Government for one dollar. The base was named after Richard Coulter Drum the Assistant Adjutant-General of the Department of the Pacific in San Francisco. It was used for training, as a supply base in the Southwest, and as Army headquarters from 1861 to1871.

The Drum Barracks hospital was recognized as the best medical facility west of the Mississippi River.

The tour guide begins with background information about the base and those who served here and prepared for war within the compound. A three-dimensional model showing details of the original site in 1863 is a focal point of this discussion. The California units who trained at this facility were recognized as some of the best equipped and trained in the area. Also in this room historical documents of interest are framed and displayed on the walls. Handwritten letters from generals and other writings document the conditions at the base as well as other historical events.

The displays upstairs include a bedroom of the time period. In the bedroom is a suite of black walnut furniture. A room across the hall depicts a Civil War period campsite. A tent, similar to one that a typical soldier would have used, is set up with a makeshift campfire. The games the soldiers would have played are also on display in this room. The checkers on the board are made of dried corn cobs. The best room upstairs would have to be the armory. The displays of guns, swords, and gear is exciting to look over. The best part of the room is the Gatling gun.

The tour continues downstairs with the famous Vicksburg battlefield flag. If this flag could tell stories it would amaze us all. The tour ends in the gift shop where the nonprofit organization sells Civil War Memorabilia.

TAKE THE TOUR

WHERE TO GO
1200 Getty Center Drive
Los Angeles, CA 90049

WHEN TO GO
Self-Guided Tours
Guided Tours
On the hour
Sunday - Thursday
10am to 6 p.m.
Friday - Saturday
10am to 9pm

DEGREE OF DIFFICULTY
Easy

CONTACT
310.440.7300
www.getty.edu

GETTY CENTER

The Getty Center, over 110 acres in Los Angeles, is an opportunity to enjoy a relaxing afternoon and explore art, architecture and horticulture. Right off the 405 freeway, visitors are taken to the Getty from the main parking lot on a small tram system that leads to the top of the mountain. At the Getty, visitors enjoy one of the best views of Los Angeles and the buildings of the complex are works of art in themselves.

Getty is mostly known for the collections in the Museum. The permanent collection includes contributions from Monet, Tiepolo, Rembrandt, and Michelangelo. There are five two story pavilions. The galleries are divided to show art from different periods and influences. For example there is a gallery of French furniture and others of impressionist paintings.

In the central plaza visitors can enjoy the dramatic architecture and gardens. In fact the entire acreage is quite unique and beyond comparison with anything else in the Los Angeles area. The Getty Center, designed by American architect Richard Meier, is constructed from Italian travertine stone. The composition of the facility is open with lines that give a sense of movement and space. Architectural tours are available daily on a first come first served basis. On the tour visitors get detailed information about the buildings and the materials used to create this magnificent place.

The Center Garden, in a natural ravine between the Museum and the Research Institute, was designed by Robert Irwin. This dramatic garden brings visitors to a new depth of understanding and experience of plants. A jagged walkway follows down the center of the planters in such a way that the entire garden can be viewed from several angles. At the end of the walkway, there is a circular garden full of blooming flowers. Inside the circle is a pool of water. Garden tours are available daily as well. The tour schedules change so visitors need to check with the information desk to get the exact times.

The Getty gives visitors many opportunities to explore with several free tours as well as a beautiful place to wonder about and soak up art and architecture.

LONG BEACH AIRPORT

On first impression, you might mistake the architecture of the Long Beach Airport to be a boat. Sculpted to look like a cruise ship, this building completed in 1941 was a tribute to the flying of the past. The terminal building is tiled with unique mosaic images including the city's seal of Long Beach is right inside the main entrance.

Before the current building was built the actual planes were found at the airport on the beach. The runway and hangers for the airplanes were on waterfront property. It was not unusual to see planes take off during low tide right over the water. With the building of the port and the popularity of flying in the area, the decision was made to move the airport inland. The Long Beach Airport, also known as Daugherty Field, is home to five runways and can handle all sizes of aircraft.

The tour of the field gives some historic insights into aviators of the past. On display are pictures, posters and historical information along the two different hallways honoring women flyers, the McDonnell Douglas Company (Long Beach's largest employer), as well as Earl Daugherty.

The tour, done especially for children, focuses on the functions of an airport. Starting on the main floor kids get the chance to understand the process of checking in for a flight. Shown the airline counters and how luggage is checked, the tour moves on to the gates. Here the kid's see how the metal detectors work and what happens when passengers walk out to the plane. Next up is a talk about the process of flying. Using models, the science of flying is explained in simple terms. Information on flying can also be found on the walls of the area. A secure balcony overlooking the runways and flight areas is where the tour ends.

Visitors don't have to be on a scheduled flight to enjoy the historic energy of aviation. The Long Beach Airport is open to the public daily for self guided tours of the exhibits on both levels.

TAKE THE TOUR

WHERE TO GO
4100 Donald Douglas Drive
Long Beach, CA 90808

WHEN TO GO
Guided Tours
Reservations Required

DEGREE OF DIFFICULTY
Moderate

CONTACT
562.570.2679
www.lgb.org

TAKE THE TOUR

WHERE TO GO
Berth 84, Foot of 6th Street
San Pedro, CA 90731

WHEN TO GO
Self-Guided Tours
Tuesday – Sunday
10am - 4:30pm

DEGREE OF DIFFICULTY
Easy

CONTACT
310.548.7618
www.lamaritimemuseum.org

LOS ANGELES MARITIME MUSEUM

The majority of goods shipped in and out of the United States pass through the Port of Los Angeles. One of the largest ports in the Western United States, the history of this area can be found only a few blocks away at the Los Angeles Maritime Museum. From the merchants to the U.S. Navy, the area has grown substantially because of the influence of the port.

The Maritime Museum offers a hands on opportunity to learn about boats, ships, sailing and the navigation of the oceans. Although the museum is small, every exhibit offers an interesting angle of maritime life. On the first floor visitors will be surprised at how many boats and ships are on display. All miniature in size, the vessels are in glass cases. Created with attention to the most minute details, the amazing part is how much can be learned from these models. In the middle of the room, the model of a cruise ship can capture the imagination for hours. With the model cut in half, the luxurious and functional structures of the ship can be seen. The details of the cruise ship are so good it is possible to see the fuzz on the carpet. Ship wheels, simple boats and ship ornaments are also on display in this area.

Up the walk way are more variations of ships. Looking out the window on the way up the stairs ships in the port can be seen. On the top floor more information about the harbor and the ships is presented. At the far window a mounted set of ship binoculars gives visitors a glimpse of the shores about a mile away.

The Los Angeles Maritime Museum captures the sea going heritage through the exhibits and a program that works with young people to preserve and build boats.

LOS ANGELES TEMPLE

Right off Santa Monica Boulevard there is a quiet place to relax and refresh at the Los Angeles Temple. The grounds of the area are exquisite and visitors will find themselves in a calming realm only miles from downtown Los Angeles. This temple is part of the Church of Jesus Christ of Latter-Day Saints.

The grounds around the temple, are open to the public daily. The grass and beautiful views are complimented by the statues. The flower garden and trees are well taken care of and quite stunning. Benches are available in several places for visitors to sit and reflect upon life.

The visitor's center across the street from the Temple offers a chance to view the 12 foot marble statue of Jesus Christ inside the main door. Other amazing statues relating to biblical times are also present for viewing. For those who decide to visit the Center or are thinking about asking for a guided tour of the grounds, it is it is important to remember that the missionaries inside are also focused on sharing their religion and that will be a significant part of the tour as well.

One interesting monument to look closer at in this area is the monument to women with several small statuettes of women in activities. The details of this area are extraordinary and worth the look.

TAKE THE TOUR

WHERE TO GO
10777 Santa Monica Blvd.
Los Angeles, CA 90025

WHEN TO GO
Self Guided Tours
9am- 9pm Daily

DEGREE OF DIFFICULTY
Moderate

CONTACT
310.475.4885
www.latemple.org

LUMMIS HOUSE

Walking around the grounds of the Lummis House, visitors can easily feel overwhelmed with all the intense work put into the home and gardens. This tour covers not only the workmanship of the house but also the impressive life of a man well known in Los Angeles.

The tour takes visitors back to the El Alisal, home of Charles Lummis, 'built to last a thousand years.' A famous author, poet and librarian, his roots in the Los Angeles area are of epic proportion. Graduating from Harvard in 1881, he published and sold 12,000 copies of his poems, printed on birch bark. In 1884, living in Cincinnati, he decided to walk 3,000 miles to Los Angeles and send detailed accounts of his progress to the Los Angeles Times. The journalistic experiment took 143 days to complete and had many readers awaiting his next account of his journey. This adventure almost cost him his life in the deep snows of New Mexico. When he finally did arrive in Los Angeles, he was made the first city editor of the Los Angeles Times.

The Lummis house was constructed over a twelve year period. The rocks came from the Arroyo Seco, a rocky riverbed running between downtown Los Angeles and Pasadena. Built outside solely of rocks and concrete, the front door of the house actually is in the middle of the yard. The design of the house was intended to show the beauty in the climate and culture of the Southwest. Visitors will see influences of Native Americans, Spanish Missions and the Southwest throughout the house.

Another important part of this tour is to walk through the gardens. This water wise garden is a display of plants appropriate for the climate of Southern California. Some are native to the area and others come from the Mediterranean. In the middle of the garden is a display giving more information about plants and the area region. The tour ends in the backyard area. Here visitors are able to see several of the extra buildings used for storing equipment.

TAKE THE TOUR

WHERE TO GO
200 East Avenue 43
Los Angeles, CA 90031

WHEN TO GO
Guided Tour
Friday - Sunday
12 noon - 4pm

DEGREE OF DIFFICULTY
Easy

CONTACT
323.222.0546

MARINE MAMMAL CARE CENTER AT FORT MACARTHUR

TAKE THE TOUR

WHERE TO GO
3601 South Gaffey Street
San Pedro, CA 90731

WHEN TO GO
Self-Guided Tours
Daylight Hours Daily

DEGREE OF DIFFICULTY
Easy

CONTACT
310.548.5677
www.mar3ine.org

Saving marine mammals is the mission of the Marine Mammal Care Center at Fort MacArthur in San Pedro. Rescuing mammals from all over the region, they focus on bringing them back to the facility with the hope of releasing them back into the wild in best of health. The job seems to be a big one as thousands of animals are hurt yearly in California boating accidents. However, saving one at a time, the trainers at this facility return many of the hurt animals to the ocean once they are well enough to brave the waves.

The opportunity to see this project in motion is one that should not be missed. Visitors get the chance to view these animals from only a few feet away (guarded by a chain link fence of course) and amazingly the animals tend to enjoy looking at the people too. There is room for at least eight animals in the facility and most of the time it is half full. Focusing on the animal's needs, the trainers tend to be occupied working with the animals, but if you ask there is a good chance they can answer questions about what they are doing.

There is no telling what animals will be in the facility and the fact that they often change makes this a great tour to attend many times. During my visit I saw a seal and a sea lion, both of which enjoyed barking at the top of their lungs. The seal was especially interested in flapping the water, splashing it everywhere.

Visitors touring the Marine Mammal Care Center, will see that California is lucky to have a top notch care facility for the ocean animals.

TAKE THE TOUR

WHERE TO GO
6400 Bixby Hill Road
Long Beach, CA 90815

WHEN TO GO
Guided Tours
Wednesday - Sunday
1 - 5pm

DEGREE OF DIFFICULTY
Easy

CONTACT
562.431.3541

RANCHO LOS ALAMITOS

Settled in the middle of a residential neighborhood, the Rancho Los Alamitos is an opportunity to reflect upon the ongoing story of Southern California's culture and environment. The history of the ranch follows the Spanish and Mexican periods, but even before then the hilltop nestled in the Long Beach area was home to Native Americans. The guided tour covers only a small portion of the 7.5 acres of the ranch. There are three interesting areas to explore after the tour so plan to visit the ranch for a couple of hours.

Starting inside on the guided tour, a docent will give a presentation about how the ranch was set up for the family who lived in the dwelling. Added on and

reworked over the years, the core of the house is a dirt wall adobe. Built around 1800 as a shelter while watching the livestock, the house was put up after a 300,000 acre land grant was given to Manuel Nieto.

In the actual adobe house, the dirt walls are still exposed. A glass covered cut out is made in the house to demonstrate how thick the walls had to be to protect the occupants from the elements. In some places the wall is over a foot thick, the other sections of the house were constructed with wood. Walking through the different rooms, appliances and gadgets are on display that require a second look to figure out their use. The lack of technology aside, the innovative way these people used to live is a fascinating part of this tour.

On the tour, pay close attention to the dining room. With the table beautifully set, the family would come here to eat three times a day. To eat a meal, they had to be dressed properly. The guide will show an interesting part of the wall where the original wallpaper was destroyed. A close look reveals how an artist carefully painted the same design in an attempt to repair the damage. Further on the tour, past the kitchen is where the work hands ate their food. The bell gave the signal for them to come in from the fields to eat.

Once back in the courtyard, visitors will be guided over to the barns. The mainstay of survival for country life in the early 1900's, agriculture was what kept the community going. The ranch produced cattle hides and tallow, selling or bartering for goods and services. The barns, all dating back to the early 1900's except one building, were traditional shapes and sizes that had colors reflecting European and Eastern traditions. The tack used on the farm for the horses and cattle is still sitting on the benches made for the equipment. The tour ends in the milking barn. The guides will show the group an interesting looking three legged stool. Visitors may want to go back and look closely at the sheep wagon or the different tools used in the blacksmith shop. As the guide is on a schedule, small items such as these have only a limited exposure before it is essential to move on.

After the tour, take some time to look at the gardens. Four acres comprise a series of beautiful gardens. Different tiers present an elegant look at how important gardens were to the daily lives of the early settlers. From the gardens, be sure to take the path to the front of the house. Standing three or four stories high, is the Moreton Bay Fig tree. The fig tree is so big that the trunk spreads out over four feet around. This tour is by far one of the best historical tours offered in the area and not to be missed.

THE WAYFARERS CHAPEL

Built on a cliff overlooking the ocean in Rancho Palos Verdes, the Wayfarers Chapel is a sight to behold. Designed by Lloyd Wright, the very talented son of famous architect Frank Lloyd Wright, the chapel is an architectural wonder of design meeting nature. All of these features make it one of the perfect settings for an afternoon outing in the Los Angeles area. The Wayfarers Chapel is like no other church, designed and built to look out into the ocean and beyond, it successfully captures the beauty of nature. The church and grounds offer wonderful places to sit and enjoy the sights.

At the visitor's center there are interesting interactive exhibits on the design and building of the church. Each piece was painstakingly placed to make a specific statement about the church and its surroundings. These exhibits exemplify the artistic qualities Lloyd Wright utilized in his design and use of material. The beautiful integration of the landscape and the architecture make the Wayfarers Chapel a popular location for weddings.

The self guided tour starts inside the chapel. The small sidewalk just above the parking lot, allows visitors to take in the beauty as they make their way into the chapel. Made almost entirely of glass, the chapel was built in 1951. Using 30 and 60 degree angles that occur in nature, instead of the common 90 degree angle used in building, Wright created a unique feel of open space flowing from the church into the world. The diamond design on the floor reflects the pattern of the ceiling which with the six acoustic triangular panels balances the sound.

The tower, finished in 1954 has a gold leaf cross fifty feet above the floor of the chapel. Calling it God's Candle, sailors using the Catalina Channel at night can see it from a distance. On your tour you may hear the bells from the belfry above ring hourly as well as at the conclusion of a wedding.

After leaving the chapel, the remainder of the tour is left to explore the grounds. Every tree and plant which decorates the grounds was an intentional part of the overall design. The Wayfarers Chapel was originally known as the 'glass church.' Later, after the foliage started growing in, the name was changed to the 'tree chapel.' Setting out to create a peaceful place in harmony with nature, original plants found in California forests and areas were seeded ultimately creating the magnificent solitude presented today.

Benches are placed around the grounds for visitors to sit and ponder. Sitting close to the meditation garden and hillside stream visitors enjoy a quiet moment to relax.

Tours FOR FREE™

CHANNEL ISLANDS MAINLAND
VISITORS CENTER

EL PRESIDIO DE SANTA BARBARA

FILLMORE FISH HATCHERY

KARPELES MANUSCRIPT
 LIBRARY MUSEUM

OLIVAS ADOBE

OXNARD HERITAGE SQUARE

RED TILE TOUR

SANTA BARBARA AIRPORT

SANTA BARBARA
COUNTY COURTHOUSE

SANTA BARBARA HISTORICAL
MUSEUM

SANTA BARBARA WINERY

VENTURA HISTORIC
WALKING TOUR

WITCH CREEK WINERY

CENTRAL COAST

CHANNEL ISLANDS MAINLAND VISITOR CENTER

TAKE THE TOUR

WHERE TO GO
1901 Spinnaker Drive
Ventura, CA 93001

WHEN TO GO
Self Guided Tour
8:30am – 5:00pm Daily

DEGREE OF DIFFICULTY
Easy

CONTACT
805.658.5730
www.nps.gov/chis

Channel Islands Mainland Visitor Center, at the foot of e Ventura Harbor, offers a great opportunity to explore d understand the ocean and the islands. Designated a ational Park, these islands play host to visitors from around the world as well as cals enjoying the splendor.

The self-guided tour at the visitor center covers the animals, plants and geology und on the islands as well as the ocean surrounding it. The only way to get to the land is by boat or plane, so the visitor's center on the mainland gives visitors a impse of all the island has to offer.

Outside the visitor center is a garden containing all the different plant species und growing on the islands. The plants vary from island to island since different rieties were introduced by settlers and diverse soil conditions affected growing atterns.

In the foyer of the visitor's center, each of the islands is displayed on a detailed map to help visitors grasp the size of the region. Above the display, a banner hangs from the ceiling highlighting some of the islands' features. The stairs up to the observation deck display actual fish and plants found during the different stages of the ocean's evolution.

On the third floor there are binoculars for getting a close-up look at the surrounding islands and Ventura Harbor. Birds, boats and waves can all be enjoyed from this spectacular vantage point and the smell of the ocean fills the air. Information boards below the binoculars offer explanations of what can be seen in all directions.

Back on the first floor, inside the visitor center, a display of the islands' ecology explains the importance of keeping the islands free of pollution. There are also interactive displays that allow visitors to touch shells, bones and other items found on the island.

EL PRESIDIO DE SANTA BARBARA

TAKE THE TOUR

WHERE TO GO
123 East Canon Perdido St.
Santa Barbara, CA 93101

WHEN TO GO
Self-Guided Tours
10:30am – 4:30pm daily

DEGREE OF DIFFICULTY
Easy

CONTACT
805.966.9719
www.sbthp.org

Located in downtown Santa Barbara, the Santa Barbara Royal Presidio played an important role in California's history. Established on April 21, 1782, it was the last of a chain of Presidios, or fortified settlements, built by the Spanish along the coast of California. Padre Junipero Serra, the man known for founding the California Missions, blessed the site.

The job of the Presidio was to protect the missions and settlers from Indian attacks and guard the territory from foreign invasion. The Presidio was the cultural and social center of the area and containing the only non-native population in the area, the military families played an important part in the colonization of California.

The tour at the Presidio covers the two remaining sections of the original site. Starting at the Canedo Adobe, visitors can see the row of rooms that once housed the Presidio soldiers and their families. The next room is the reconstructed office and bedroom reserved for chaplains. Appropriately named the Padre's Quarters, this room dates back to the Spanish colonial period.

The chapel is by far the most beautiful of the reconstructed buildings. Only the stone foundation of the chapel is original, but excavations and historic records made reconstruction of the building possible. The inside of the chapel was restored with such care and attention that it transports the visitor back in time.

The tour ends across the street at the only surviving structure in a row of family living quarters called the El Cuartel. Each room housed an entire family and the row extended along the entire western side of the Presidio. The El Cuartel is the oldest adobe building in Santa Barbara.

TAKE THE TOUR

WHERE TO GO
612 East Telegraph Road
Fillmore, CA 93102

WHEN TO GO
Self-Guided Tours
8am – 3:30pm daily

DEGREE OF DIFFICULTY
Easy

CONTACT
805.524.0962

INTERESTING FACT:
2,000 pounds of food are
fed to the fish at the Fillmore
Fish Hatchery each day.

FILLMORE FISH HATCHERY

Only 10 minutes from Six Flags, the tour of the Fillmore Fish Hatchery is the place to see how fish are raised for use in stocking the rivers, reservoirs and lakes of California. The fish from this hatchery keep 40 state waterways stocked with trout and is a great chance to see aquiculture in action.

The hatchery has several aquariums that house fish of different sizes. The fish are raised from eggs brought in from outside sources. Once hatched, the fish are fed daily until they grow to approximately 9 to 12 inches long before being released into the wild. Keeping the fish healthy by maintaining a consistent living environment free from disease is important for the hatchery. Also, keeping the excited sea gulls and other birds that hang around this captive food source from picking up a free lunch is essential. There are large bird nests across the roof and sides of the building. While some holes are present, only a few birds have made their way in for a free meal.

As the fish grow they become strong and healthy and are moved from tank to tank as they progress in different stages of development. Unlike a home aquarium or those for public display, these aquariums have cement sides and are only 2 to 3 feet deep with an open top. The open top lets visitors look straight down at the fish. When visitors gather to look into the tank, the fish actually start jumping up toward the surface and crowd around each other to get a look and, possibly, something to eat. For those who feel like feeding the fish, there are machines along the side of the aquariums to purchase a handful of food for a quarter.

The outside bulletin board has postings with details on the actual feeding and raising of trout. There are color photographs that explain the function of a hatchery with step-by-step information.

KARPELES MANUSCRIPT LIBRARY MUSEUM

The Karpeles Manuscript Library Museum is a tour in which visitors get to view rare and historical documents such as original manuscripts and personal correspondence on display under protective glass. Historians are always faced with being able to prove that the information they report is factual. The only way to document these historic facts is through research. The best materials are primary sources which include first person accounts, diaries, ledgers and correspondence.

Many documents are on display - some alone, under glass, others in exhibits containing other pertinent items. Visitors are welcome to wander around and look at the hand written or typewritten documents and read from original letters written by famous figures like John Hancock.

The small size of the facility is no reflection of the number of topics covered in these documents. A display that honors the writing of Shakespeare and a temporary display of letters from the personal collection of Evita Peron are but a few examples of the topics covered. While some items on display are from the permanent collection, the majority of material rotates from the collections of seven other historic manuscript museums around the country.

The details about people's lives found on these documents are far more interesting to read than a historian's interpretation. The authors and their thoughts are more immediate and virtually come to life in their original writing.

TAKE THE TOUR

WHERE TO GO
21 West Anapamu Street
Santa Barbara, CA 93101

WHEN TO GO
Self-Guided Tours
10am – 4pm Daily

DEGREE OF DIFFICULTY
Easy

CONTACT
805.962.5322
www.karpeles.com

TAKE THE TOUR

WHERE TO GO
4200 Olivas Park Drive
Ventura, CA 93003

WHEN TO GO
Guided Tours
Saturday - Sunday 10am-4pm

DEGREE OF DIFFICULTY
Easy

CONTACT
805.644.4346

OLIVAS ADOBE

Just south of Ventura, the Olivas Adobe is a historic guided tour worth a visit. The building of the rancho was started in 1847, with Chumash labor. The Mexican Governor, Juan Alvorado, gave Don Raymundo the 4,693-acre ranch. Raymundo felt that it was only fitting to put a large house on the property, since this was to be a welcoming place for guests when they came through the area.

The Raymundo family made considerable money during the California Gold Rush by selling cattle to the miners until a drought destroyed the Southern California cattle industry in 1862. Raymundo rebuilt the family fortune by raising sheep.

The tour of the house consists of several different rooms in the tradition of the rancho in its glory days. Visitors are greeted by a beautiful courtyard, the centerpiece of which is a beehive oven. Commonly used to bake bread, this type of oven used to be found all over California in the 1800s.

Inside the house, visitors are guided through the different rooms, including a parlor where visitors were greeted and entertained. Music, conversation and even cards helped pass the time when friends came calling. U.S. Senator Thomas Bard was among the distinguished guests entertained here.

The bedrooms upstairs where Don Raymundo's eight daughters slept have a warm, personal feel to them, as does Raymundo's own room. Because most of the cooking was done outdoors, the kitchen is rather sparse, despite its daily use.

The Fleischmann Foundation, founded by Major Max Fleischmann of the Fleischmann Yeast and Margarine Company, gave the adobe to the City of San Buenaventura after the land had changed hands several times. After his death it was donated for the use of the general public.

OXNARD HERITAGE SQUARE

The block of buildings at Heritage Square is as diverse as the Oxnard community itself. The historic nature of the square gives visitors a chance to see what it was like to live in this seaside community more than 100 years ago. Not all the buildings are original, some are replicas made from referencing documents and photographs. The church and two of the houses are original and date from the early 1900's. The other buildings were moved from various ranches to this location.

Visitors are welcome to view the courtyard that connects all the buildings, but only these on guided tours are allowed to go through the buildings. Currently the buildings are occupied by businesses and community organizations, but plaques outside offer enough information to make a walking tour interesting.

The guided tour starts at the information center in the center of the block. From there a docent leads the tour through and around the different buildings. The entire tour follows the brick pathways and the gardens to explore the entire block. Beautifully done, the time on the tour slips quickly away with every intriguing turn.

The Pfeiler Water Tower, right across from the information center, is a replica of the original that stood at the Pfeiler Ranch House. Further down the street are the Petre Ranch House, the Scarlett House and the Connelly Ranch house. Each is an elaborate building and full of rich history. The Maulhardt House is only a replica of the original house.

Walking around on the tour, keep an eye out for the house with one eyebrow and the house with a witch cap. The guide will give more information about these distinct architectural flaws.

TAKE THE TOUR	
WHERE TO GO	715 South A Street Oxnard, CA 93030
WHEN TO GO	*Guided Tours* Saturday 10am and 2pm
DEGREE OF DIFFICULTY	Easy
CONTACT	805.483.7960

RED TILE TOUR

TAKE THE TOUR

WHERE TO GO
1 Garden Street
Santa Barbara, CA 93101

WHEN TO GO
Self-Guided Tours
9am – 3pm Daily

DEGREE OF DIFFICULTY
Easy

CONTACT
805.965.3021

To share the rich culture of the community with all who visit, the Santa Baraba Chamber of Commerce has put together a self-guided walking tour through downtown that combines historic landmarks and notable buildings. The tour map is available free at the visitor center at One Garden Street, only a block from the ocean.

The tour begins at the Santa Barbara County Courthouse where visitors can go to the top floor and look out over the city. On a clear day, it is possible to see for miles. Walking across the street, the tour continues at the Santa Barbara Public Library. Inside, paintings from the Faulkner Gallery are on exhibit. The next stop is the downtown plaza where the city's first wooden floor can by seen at the Hill-Carrillo Adobe. The beautiful Presidio Gardens is a great place to stop, take a break and soak up the latest blooms. The final stop is the historic Lobero Theatre, built in 1873 by an Italian Musician, Jose Lobero, who contributed much to the Santa Barbara music community.

SANTA BARBARA AIRPORT

TAKE THE TOUR

WHERE TO GO
45 Hartley Place
Santa Barbara, CA 93117

WHEN TO GO
Guided Tours
Reservations Required

DEGREE OF DIFFICULTY
Easy

CONTACT
805.964.7622
www.flysba.com/html/tours.html

Playing host to several local flying clubs every month, a tour of the Santa Barbara Airport offers a chance for visitors to learn more about aviation. The main building, formerly a fire station for the airport, has a great layout for tours with the bay that once housed fire trucks now used as exhibit space.

The exhibit covers the basic flow of operations at an airport, giving kids and adults alike an idea of what is involved when they take a plane somewhere. Another display focuses on how all the parts of an airport work, from a fire station to different types of airplanes.

This hands-on learning in the exhibit hall gives an understanding of the principles of flight and a working wind tunnel allows students to fly a radio controlled plane in an enclosed space. It is an identical copy of a similar exhibit at the Smithsonian Air and Space Museum. Using math and science, kids are challenged to understand the principles of flight and the operation of an airport.

Another popular part of the airport tour is the video collection. More than 200 videos on aviation history comprise the largest collection in Southern California.

SANTA BARBARA COUNTY COURTHOUSE

TAKE THE TOUR

WHERE TO GO
1100 Anacapa Street
Santa Barbara, CA 93101

WHEN TO GO
Guided Tours
Monday, Tuesday, & Friday
10:30am
Monday – Saturday 2pm

DEGREE OF DIFFICULTY
Moderate

CONTACT
805.962.6464
www.santabarbaracourthouse.org

Although the earthquake of 1925 destroyed the original Santa Barbara Courthouse, it led to the creation of one of the most beautiful buildings in the world. Devastated by the earthquake, much of the city block had to be rebuilt. An architect by the name of William Mooser convinced the city of Santa Barbara to replace its courthouse with a Mediterranean style building. Completed in 1929, the cost of the steel framed building was an enormous $1.5 million dollars. Known around the world as an artistic triumph, visitors and locals love the tour of this site.

Guided tours of the courthouse are given every day except Sunday. For those who would rather do it themselves, there is a brochure available at the information desk for a self-guided tour. Some of the striking sights on this tour include the colorful tiles that surround the entryway and the grand staircase up to the second floor.

The old Board of Supervisors assembly room holds an historic mural that depicts the history of our country. It begins with Native Americans who came to California, followed by the arrival of the first Europeans and the statehood of California. The scenes in this room are overwhelming and beautifully rendered. It is a great idea to spend a few extra minutes after the tour, coming back and closely looking at the detailed illustrations.

The tour ends with El Mirador, the clock tower. Going up the elevator, visitors can look out over the city of Santa Barbara from the deck 85 feet off the ground. This provides an unforgettable view of the city, coastline and ocean on sunny days.

SANTA BARBARA HISTORICAL MUSEUM

TAKE THE TOUR

WHERE TO GO
136 East De la Guerra St.
Santa Barbara, CA 93101

WHEN TO GO
Guided Tours
Wednesday 1:30pm
Saturday 11:30am
Sunday 1:30pm
Museum hours
Tuesday-Saturday 10am-5pm
Sunday 12noon-5pm

DEGREE OF DIFFICULTY
Easy

CONTACT
805.966.1601

The Santa Barbara Historical Museum is only a block away from the El Presidio of Santa Barbara. The U-shaped building housing the museum reflects the early style of a California home. Made out of 70,000 adobe bricks manufactured on site, the clay roof tiles make the place look more like a home than a museum.

Inside is an amazing number and variety of local artifacts. The Santa Ynez Turnpike Road sign harkens back to 1869 when residents of Santa Barbara paid to build a toll road over the San Marcos Pass. The man in charge of the pass, Patrick Kinevan, collected the money at the top of the mountain where the road crossed his ranch. The toll road was used until 1898 when the county purchased the road and opened it up to the public at no charge. Stagecoaches operated in Santa Barbara until 1901, when the railroad connecting Santa Barbara and San Francisco was finally completed.

The Gold Stamp Mill in the courtyard is another place worth a stop. Gold was discovered in Santa Barbara in 1820. This gold stamp mill was used at the Castaic Mines in Ventura in 1911. Records show that Santa Barbara sent 20 ounces of gold to the Philadelphia Mint in 1824.

At the back of the museum is the historic L-shaped Casa Covarrubias adobe built in 1817. A monument commemorating one of its former owners, Don Jose Maria Covarrubias, a distinguished California legislator, is here, too.

At the front of the museum, the exhibit hall always has something new on display. From western portraits to sculpture, there is always something new to keep visitors coming back.

SANTA BARBARA WINERY

TAKE THE TOUR

WHERE TO GO
202 Abacapa Street
Santa Barbara, CA 93101

WHEN TO GO
Guided Tours
11:30am & 3:30pm Daily

DEGREE OF DIFFICULTY
Easy

CONTACT
805.963.3633
www.sbwinery.com

Only a few blocks from the ocean, the 38-year-old Santa Barbara Winery is a picturesque operation that produces notable wines from grapes grown in the area. Inside the winery, oak aging barrels are lined up against the far wall. A counter divides the production facility and the small store where wine is for sale.

The tour covers the entire wine making process with the guide explaining each process in detail. The tour demonstrates containers used for fermenting and the barrels used to age the wine. After aging, the wines are poured into bottles, corked, labeled, and are ready to be enjoyed.

The tour is great for those spending the day in the area who would be interested in learning more about wine.

VENTURA HISTORIC WALKING TOUR

TAKE THE TOUR

WHERE TO GO
89 South California
Ventura, CA 93001

WHEN TO GO
Self-Guided Tours
Daily

DEGREE OF DIFFICULTY
Easy

CONTACT
805.648.2075

Downtown Ventura is well known for the great bargains to be found there. Whether at the thrift stores or the antique shops, people from all over Southern California flock here to shop and enjoy the city. However, a less well known but equally good reason to visit the city is the historic walking tour coordinated by the Ventura Visitors and Convention Bureau.

Covering more than 30 buildings within a six block walk, the tour begins at the Ventura County Museum of History and Art on Main Street. Introducing visitors to the life and story of Ventura County, displays focus on Native Americans, Spanish and Mexican Pioneers as well as European and East Coast Settlers. After this introduction to the region, the tour moves on to the big Moreton Bay Fig Tree located west of Figueroa Plaza. Planted more than 120 years ago, this tree was once part of the Old Mission Gardens.

The walk around downtown highlights various areas of interest, from the Bank of Italy to the Hotel Ventura. One of the highlights is the Post Office on East Main Street, built in 1861. The story goes that the city's first postmaster carried letters in his hat for delivery. This system is believed to be the first involving letter carrying in the state. On the floors the discolored outline where the original post office counter was located can be seen.

The walking tour winds around downtown ending at the Ventura City Hall. Formerly the Ventura County Courthouse, this building was designed by noted Los Angeles architect Albert Martin in 1912. This massive structure stands on top of a small hill and is graced with beautiful landscaping. Just below City Hall is a sculpture of the mission founder, Fray Junipero Serra. Constructed as part of the Federal Art Project (a division of the Works Progress Administration) in 1936, the sculpture is lifelike and fits the setting perfectly.

WITCH CREEK WINERY

TAKE THE TOUR

WHERE TO GO
2906 Carlsbad Blvd.
Carlsbad, CA 92008

WHEN TO GO
Self-Guided Tours
11am – 5pm daily

DEGREE OF DIFFICULTY
Easy

CONTACT
760.720.7499
www.witchcreekwinery.com

Only two blocks from the ocean, Witch Creek Winery is a place to discover another of Southern California's delicious wines. Named after the small creek that ran by the vintner's house in Southern California, the wines produced here are award winners as attested to by the medals on the walls. The winery kept the original Witch Creek name after the owners moved to Carlsbad.

Walking into the winery, visitors are greeted by the delicious scent of fermenting wine emanating from the barrels just inside the door. More than a dozen barrels are set off to the side for easier viewing. The vintner explains the entire process of making wine and ends his talk with a tasting. One impressive element of the Witch Creek Winery tour is the enthusiasm of the staff. They were genuinely excited about giving the tour and happy to have visitors looking around.

Focusing on quality over quantity, the winery produces small batches of fruit wines, as well as traditional grape wines, on a regular basis.

Tours FOR **FREE**™

CALIFORNIA MUSEUM OF PHOTOGRAPHY

FLEETWOOD RV

GRABER OLIVE HOUSE

HISTORICAL GLASS MUSEUM

LINCOLN MEMORIAL SHRINE

MARCH AFB FIELD MUSEUM

SILVERCREST HOMES

WORKMAN AND TEMPLE FAMILY HOMESTEAD MUSEUM

INLAND EMPIRE

CALIFORNIA MUSEUM OF PHOTOGRAPHY

TAKE THE TOUR

WHERE TO GO
3824 Main Street
Riverside, CA 92501

WHEN TO GO
Self-Guided Tours
Tuesday – Saturday
11am - 5pm

DEGREE OF DIFFICULTY
Easy

CONTACT
909.784.FOTO
www.cmp.ucr.edu

For people who love to snap shots of everything and everyone, the interesting exhibits found at the California Museum of Photography are a must see. Located at the University of California Riverside, the museum is in historic downtown Riverside on the pedestrian mall.
The displays include photographs and information about photography. One of the

displays includes one of the first motion picture cameras. Weighing in at 800 pounds, this single piece of equipment required a crew of operators just to get it to the movie set.

Exhibits change periodically, but all focus on a particular photographer or theme, so visitors get an in-depth look at a given subject or topic. Seeing a series of images by a particular photographer, and reading about what he or she was thinking, how he or she approached the craft and what his or her goals were, affords a rare opportunity to go beyond the art and into the creation.

For visitors who want the chance to understand the principals of a camera, the third floor outside exhibit called Camera Obscura is a great learning tool. This exhibit gives a view of the world from the inside of a camera – literally. Using a small lens, the image of the building across the street is transmitted onto the wall in the same way an image in a camera is captured on film. Visitors will notice some of the interesting effects a lens has on the image. This is the same process that was used to capture images of treasured paintings.

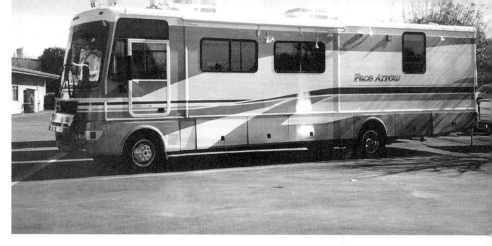

FLEETWOOD RV

TAKE THE TOUR

WHERE TO GO
5300 Via Ricardo Road
Riverside, CA 92517

WHEN TO GO
Guided Tour
Reservations Required

DEGREE OF DIFFICULTY
Easy

CONTACT
909.788.2920
www.fleetwood.com

The tour at the Fleetwood Recreational Vehicle manufacturing plant is a real eye opener on how a motor home is manufactured. The tour takes several hours and goes from the bare basics of the chassis to the finished coach ready to drive down the highway. More than 20 units are made a week, sometimes less depending on demand.

Each unit takes several weeks to build. Working from plans, the basics of each RV are put together on a moving

assembly line. Building from the bottom up, the frame and drive train are first, followed by wiring and plumbing. Then the main appliances and furnishings like sinks and walls are installed. Most of the parts are made by employees on a carpenter line in the center of the building and brought over for installation.

Once the majority of the inside necessities are in place, the siding is put on. At any one time there are seven to 10 employees working on the motor home. Finally the roof is placed on top and the unit is ready for a trip through the painting booth. The next step is the most important: quality control. The entire unit is checked with attention paid to all the working parts large and small. Every system is checked, from the water systems to the engine to the carpet and the paint, everything must be perfect. The end of the production line sees the new RV washed and placed on the finished section. Motor homes, all the different varieties Fleetwood makes, are lined up ready for shipment to dealers and direct to customers.

The inside of an RV can be customized in a variety of ways to fit a customer's needs. Appliances, electronic equipment and colors are all options that can be customized.

GRABER OLIVE HOUSE

Located just minutes from the Ontario Airport, visitors can take a tour that highlights one of the smallest fruits, the olive. The Graber Olive Company is the oldest olive packer in California, growing and producing olives since 1894 in the Los Angeles area and around the world.

Olives are bitter right off the tree and need a lot of care before they become the tasty fruit found on the grocers' shelves. There is an elaborate process that the olives must go though before being packed and shipped. This process is what the Graber Olive Company tour is all about.

The tour begins with the olives in bins. Picked North of Los Angeles then trucked to the plant, the olives are readied for production in the early hours of the morning. Olives come in many different colors, but the majority are either green or black after they are cured. The olives from Graber are light red when picked and turn a light greenish-brown after they are cured. To keep quality high, the pickers only harvest a few olives from each tree at a time and carefully place them in velvet-lined buckets. The olives are then separated by size and placed on a belt with a slot in it. They roll down a slight incline and the slots in the belt get gradually wider. When they fall through into bins below, they are collected by size. Employees stand on each side of the belt picking out debris, under-ripe and overripe olives. After they are sized, the olives are put into round concrete vats with a curing liquid and they remain there, being stirred daily, for three weeks. The curing liquid is the secret to a perfect olive and Graber guards its recipe well. The liquid varies from company to company giving each company's brand its own unique flavor. Unlike other brands, the olives at Graber are so soft they can't be pitted without destroying them. This eliminates the pitting process, a major step in production found at other olive producers.

Once ready for eating, the olives are canned. Each can is filled by hand to ensure the olives are not damaged. As the cans are sealed, they are placed into a cart and rolled into a boiler room where they stay for over an hour to pasteurize. The final stop is the labeling machine. The cans are then placed into cases for shipping.

The tour is available year round, but visitors can see the complete canning process only during the fall harvest season. After the tour, don't forget to stop in the gift shop for a free sample and, if you like what you taste, pick up a can or two for the road. Outside of the gift shop and production facility is a small park. Here visitors can relax under the fruit trees and explore the old farming equipment on display.

HISTORICAL GLASS MUSEUM

The fine craftsmanship and attention to detail that can be seen in the glass work of yesteryear makes a fascinating tour at the Historic Glass Museum. From the fine glass works of the 1800's to the better-known Depression Glass of the 1930s, the collection includes a wide variety of pieces in its exhibit.

The collection of pieces is quite extensive due to the fact that museum members and friends of the museum have donated most of the glass. The intimate involvement of the members in the collection is evident from the interest and enthusiasm demonstrated by the staff that runs the museum. It is clear that staff knows all of the exhibited pieces well and may have even had the piece in their own home at one point. Opened in 1985, the museum was nine years in the making. The building in which the museum is housed is actually a 1903 Victorian style house and former home of Emma Cryer, daughter of early Redlands settlers Jerome and Martha Seymour. The pieces on display include candlesticks, milk glass, bowls and antique plates. The museum displays cards explaining each piece and its origin, plus the staff is always available to add details or stories about a particular piece.

There are many unusual glassworks at this museum including a glass clothes iron. Made primarily out of glass, it looks similar to the electric irons used today except it is much more artistic. Another interesting piece is the opalescent glass swan that beautiful to behold as well as an impressive 1800's punch bowl. Other items include a human hair wreath made from locks of hair from each of the Seymours as a tribute to the family. It hangs next to the door and is thought to bring prosperity and fortune.

While visiting the museum, don't forget to see the items from the estate of the famous pianist Liberace. A large glass platter with flying butterflies cut into the center is on exhibit as well as Liberace's glass compote used to hold candy at his home.

TAKE THE TOUR

WHERE TO GO
125 W. Vine Street
Redlands, CA 92373

WHEN TO GO
Self Guided Tours
Tuesday – Sunday 1-5pm

DEGREE OF DIFFICULTY
Easy

CONTACT
909.798.7632

LINCOLN MEMORIAL SHRINE

Built in 1932, the Lincoln Shrine is the only such memorial dedicated to the president West of the Mississippi River. While this is a self-guided tour, docents are available to answer questions and their knowledge adds much to the experience.

The outside of the building is constructed of reinforced concrete faced with Bedford Indiana limestone plates, which are inscribed with excerpts from Lincoln's speeches. The building is an octagon with subsequent additions that allowed the collection to grow.

One of the best parts of this tour are the beautiful murals that depict Abraham Lincoln before, during and after his presidency.

In addition to being a shrine this tour is an important place to find information about Lincoln and the Civil War. From exhibits on the Civil War to the president's personal artifacts, visitors are presented with detailed images and information making it easy to understand this important figure in our nation's history.

A display about the penny discusses how the choice of images of his face was decided upon.

MARCH AIR FORCE BASE FIELD MUSEUM

TAKE THE TOUR

WHERE TO GO
Van Buren Blvd off ramp
on I -215
March Air Reserve Base, CA
92518

WHEN TO GO
Self Guided Tours
10am – 5pm Daily

DEGREE OF DIFFICULTY
Moderate

CONTACT
909.697.6600
www.rth.org/march

For anyone who has ever dreamed of flying, or is simply fascinated with airplanes, the tour of the March Air Force Base Field Museum is a fabulous place to explore. Just off of Interstate 215, visitors can get up close and touch these well preserved airplanes of March Air Force Base Field Museum. The museum is home to the fastest plane ever built, the SR-17 Blackbird, and more than 2,000 artifacts.

Before entering the museum, inside a courtyard, the West Coast National War Dog Memorial is a good introduction to the lives of those who actually made these planes famous. Also in this area, the P-38 National Association Memorial, the 15 Air Force Memorial Wall and the Freedom Shrine are important stops on the tour. Each of these memorials depicts important parts of aviation and military history.

The exhibits are divided into time frames and battles, showing the actual planes that fought during the various wars. The purpose of each plane, the role it played and the tactical accomplishments are outlined in the exhibits. World War I and II and the Korean War have several exhibits to highlight important moments and people in those campaigns. Women aviators and the function and purpose of each plane's armaments is also discussed. One thing that strikes a visitor to this museum is how very rapidly aviation technology progressed since the Wright Brother's famous flight in 1903.

SILVERCREST HOMES FACTORY TOUR

TAKE THE TOUR

WHERE TO GO
299 N. Smith Avenue
Corona, CA 91720

WHEN TO GO
Guided Tours
Saturday 10 am

DEGREE OF DIFFICULTY
Moderate

CONTACT
1.800.382.0709
www.silvercrest-rv.com

Once a week, visitors are allowed to visit the production line of SilverCrest Homes. Building one- and two-story manufactured homes, this tour gives a behind-the-scenes look at the processes that go into making the manufactured homes of today. A home built start to finish usually takes three to four weeks, depending on the number of orders for the month.

SilverCrest makes manufactured homes primarily for the Western United States and Southern California, but their products can be found as far East as Colorado.

The tour starts off explaining how the plans for a custom home are selected. An individual picks a floor plan, decides on colors and other decorative options and the home starts down the production line.

The tour starts with an introduction to the two parts of a manufactured home, the actual construction of the exterior and the assembly of the interior elements such as walls, kitchen cabinets, bathrooms and closets. These two processes are going on at the plant simultaneously.

A manufactured home starts with a chassis. This is where the home will connect with the foundation and, unlike earlier "mobile homes," this long, solid piece, becomes the floor. Wheels are only temporarily attached in order to move the home to its future location. Once the home is delivered to the lot, the tires are removed and the rims are blocked to secure the unit.

Once the floor is in place, up go the walls. Lifted with a crane, the wood for the walls is lifted and nailed into place. Depending on if it is a single, double or triple-wide unit, the walls could be entire plywood sheets or several sheets put together. Next comes the interior. The items built on the second lines are now inserted into the home as requested by the purchaser. Craftsmen build shelves, closets, cabinets and other items that are fitted to the specific model being built. From cabinets to plumbing, the functional interior is readied.

As the unit is moved down the line, it has anywhere from six to twelve people working on it at a time, each focusing on his or her part and working quickly. Finally the unit is roofed and carpeted.

The second half of the tour focuses on the homes outside. In various stages, guides will point out different styles and options available when purchasing a home. The final product can be seen in the various models on display that are ready to be towed to their new owners.

This is an informative tour for anyone interested in construction, home improvements or buying a manufactured home. Some highlights include a discussion of the drawbacks of plastic pipes verses copper pipes or the type of glue the manufacturing housing industry uses for putting together a home.

TAKE THE TOUR

WHERE TO GO
15415 East Don Julian Road
City of Industry, CA 91745

WHEN TO GO
Guided Tours
Wednesday – Sunday
1 - 4pm

DEGREE OF DIFFICULTY
Moderate

CONTACT
626.968.8492
www.homesteadmuseum.org

WORKMAN AND TEMPLE FAMILY HOMESTEAD MUSEUM

The Workman and Temple Family Homestead is a chance to see more than 100 years of evolving California history, detailed accounts of the Mexican-American War and the growth of Los Angeles into a major metropolis. In about an hour, visitors are guided through the Workman house, the Spanish Colonial revival home "La Casa Nueva" and the outdoor gardens.

The Workman family moved to California to flee turmoil in the Texas territory during the war with Mexico. Buying land from the Mexican governor in 1842, an adobe was built by William and Nicolasa Workman. The nationality of the home changed when Los Angeles was claimed by the United States. The Workman's had been successful during the gold rush selling beef and supplies to the prospectors. The 1920's house is a mansion noted for the architectural nature of the times.

The tour gives detailed accounts of day-to-day life during different times in the history of the property. From the mud walls of the original Spanish adobe to the decorative interiors of the 1920's mansion, this tour brings the history of the homestead alive. As visitors step inside the mansion, the lavish furniture and tasteful décor is a sight to behold. There are two floors of stained glass windows. Of special note are the depictions of noted composers on the panes of the music room windows and the foyer stain glass displaying the likenesses of the two Temple children.

Outside the homes, a highly decorated landscape is a treat for the eye. The walkway in front of the Spanish home has the names of all the missions in the area carefully placed upon the sidewalk. Following along, visitors end up at the front of the ranch where the ranch brand is placed on the sidewalk.

Covering six-acres, the ranch was bought by the City of Industry to share with the people of the community. Docent-lead tours help visitors learn about the rich history of these homes. Highlighting the people and the community of yesteryear, visitors are able to experience the wonder of California in this educational and entertaining tour.

Tours FOR **FREE**™

HERITAGE HILL
HISTORICAL PARK

ORANGE COUNTY
PERFORMING ARTS CENTER

ORANGE COUNTY REGISTER

ORANGE COUNTY

TAKE THE TOUR

WHERE TO GO
25151 Serrano Road
Lake Forest, CA 92630

WHEN TO GO
Guided Tours
Wednesday – Friday 2
Saturday - Sunday 11, 2

DEGREE OF DIFFICULTY
Moderate

CONTACT
949.855.2028
www.ocparks.com/heritagehill

HERITAGE HILL HISTORICAL PARK

Located in Lake Forest, this Historical Landmark is Orange County's first historical park. The displays at the park tie the history of the region together, from the Mexican Rancheros of the 1800s to the beginning of the citrus industry in the 1920s.

Starting at the Serrano Adobe, built by Don Jose Serrano in 1863, the original land of this rancho was 10,688 acres. There were five adobes built, but the Serrano Adobe is the only remaining building. A warm house with a beautiful porch, the structure is in good condition and offers a rare opportunity to see how homes in the mid-1800s were designed and constructed.

Another important stop on the tour is the St. George's Episcopal Mission. Most of the inside furniture is original, with hand carved benches and a reed organ for music. The church, originally located on Whisler Drive in El Torro, is all that is left of the English colony.

Stepping over to the El Torro Grammar School, this one room schoolhouse was built in 1890. Used until 1914, it was located on the west corner of First Street and Olive Avenue. Stepping inside is like going back in time 100 years. The desks are perfectly lined up with schoolbooks ready to read. Assignments for the children are written on the blackboards.

Another place to visit is the Bennett Ranch House. Built in 1908 on the corner of 2nd and Cherry avenues, this is the only remaining turn-of-the-century house in El Torro. Charles Bennett, original owner of the house, purchased land to become a citrus farmer. Pursuing citrus farming for the ranch was a full time job as Charles Bennett's son Harvey joined the farm when the elder Bennett became ill.

TAKE THE TOUR

WHERE TO GO
600 Town Center Drive
Costa Mesa, CA 92626

WHEN TO GO
Guided Tours
Wednesday, Saturday 10:30

DEGREE OF DIFFICULTY
Moderate

CONTACT
714.556-2122 ext. 259
www.ocpac.org/about/tourinfo.asp

ORANGE COUNTY PERFORMING ARTS CENTER

Catering to the performing arts of the community, the Orange County Performing Arts Center brings music from around the world to locals and visitors. Home of the Pacific Symphony Orchestra, the Philharmonic Society of Orange County, Opera Pacific, the William Hall Master Chorale and the Pacific Chorale this non-profit facility is a vast complex and covers many types of performing arts.

The guided tours are given by the center docents, who are well versed in the performing arts and the center. As the tour moves about the building, visitors are given the chance to explore the huge structure and the art within. From the hallways into the exhibit hall, the attention paid to the ambiance is obvious.

The architecture integrates the function of acoustics with a beautiful and interesting design. The guides offer information and stories about the various forms of visual art that complement the décor of the lobby and other areas of the Center. The heart of the Center is in the immense talent of the performers who have graced its stage. More than 70 Broadway musicals have been performed here as well as top entertainers such as Julio Iglesias, Andy Williams, Tony Bennett, and Mel Torme.

The outside of the building is sculpted in such a way that visitors will find themselves in a slanted maze of bushes. The art in front of the building also shows how much of an influence the art has on the community.

ORANGE COUNTY REGISTER

TAKE THE TOUR

WHERE TO GO
625 North Grand
Santa Ana, CA 92701

WHEN TO GO
Guided Tours
Reservations Required

DEGREE OF DIFFICULTY
Easy

CONTACT
714.796.7000
www.ocregister.com

Located just off the 405 freeway in Santa Ana, the Orange County Register newspaper has been reporting the news since 1905. The tour of this Pulitzer Prize-winning paper and its printing plant is a good introduction to the newspaper industry. Along the walls, visitors get to see several striking and prize-winning images taken by the photographers who work at the newspaper.

From the beginning, visitors know that the reporters cover a variety of beats. Because every reporter is searching for a news story, the idea of covering only a certain issue makes it easier for the reporters to do their job. Once the reporter finds a story, the idea is relayed back to the editor in charge of the section. If the editor feels the story is important enough, the reporter is assigned to the story and starts reporting and writing. The editors decide exactly where a story will run in a newspaper and what kind of play it receives from the front page to the inside, or just a brief. The coverage all depends on how important the story is to the readers. Once the story has been written and edited, it is sent to a copy editor who makes sure the story is grammatically perfect.

Sometimes a story needs photographs to help show readers what the reporter is talking about or what someone looks like. Visitors get to see the photo department where film is developed and placed on light tables to be chosen for the specific story. Taking an average of 20 pictures for every one used in the newspaper, rolls of film are constantly being developed in the big machine along the wall.

After the editorial process is complete, the production of the newspaper starts. The tour guide will point out how negative images are made of the pages to be printed. Each page is laid out and the design and graphics decided upon before the actual story is written. This is done to accommodate the advertisements on each page. Once the negative is made, which looks just like film in a regular camera, an aluminum plate is imprinted with the negative image for use on the presses.

The final stop on the tour is the pressroom where the four-floor press is viewed from above. Watching how fast the newspaper runs through the presses is amazing. At the bottom of the stairs and out the door, visitors can see the newspapers being threaded through the wall to the bundling machines. The carriers are responsible for combining the newspaper sections and advertisements of each paper. They are given all the sections of the paper to put together to deliver on time.

ANTIQUE GAS AND
STEAM ENGINE MUSEUM

BATES NUT FARM

BELL GARDENS

BUENA VISTA AUDUBON NATURE
CENTER

CALIFORNIA SURF MUSEUM

CALLAWAY GOLF BALLS

CALLAWAY GOLF CLUBS

LAWRENCE WELK MUSEUM

NATIONAL RV FACTORY TOUR

ORFILA VINEYARDS

TAYLOR MADE ADIDUS GOLF

WINCHESTER CHEESE

ANTIQUE GAS AND STEAM ENGINE MUSEUM

TAKE THE TOUR

WHERE TO GO
2040 North Santa Fe Ave.
Vista, CA 92083

WHEN TO GO
Self-Guided
Daily 10am to 4pm

DEGREE OF DIFFICULTY
Easy

CONTACT
760.941.1791
www.agsem.com

California's past comes alive at the Antique Gas and Steam Engine Museum. On display are more than 300 pieces of equipment, including tractors, wagons, oil wells and an array of farming equipment. The museum is set up to recreate the feeling of a working farm. Visitors get the chance to see furnished barns, the farmhouse and the trappings of a way of life that only your grandmother would recognize.

The self-guided tour begins inside the gate of the museum. The historic tractors parked in the barns give a good feel for how these labor saving machines developed over the years. From the shiny green vintage John Deere to the later International tractor, the design of each model improves in form and function over time. Before internal combustion engines were invented, horse-drawn equipment was the only way to work the land. When gas and steam engines were

introduced, they provided a significant increase in productivity while reducing the labor needed. It is especially interesting to see the different wheels used on the earlier models of the different tractors. From solid iron tracks to tires on rims, the size and shape changed as new materials were developed.

The oil wells are another interesting part of the exhibit. The simple design of the oil well improved as oil drilling became more essential. The "bobbing horse head" design is one of the consistent features of the oil well and is still used today.

This tour offers a great opportunity to think about all that California had to offer to the early settlers and the challenges they faced in working the land. All around the yard, gas and steam engine equipment provide links to the past that are both educational and interesting. Bring a camera and enjoy the day.

Bates Nut Farm

BATES NUT FARM

TAKE THE TOUR

WHERE TO GO
15954 Woods Valley Road
Valley Center, CA 92082

WHEN TO GO
Self-Guided Tour
9am-5pm daily

DEGREE OF DIFFICULTY
Easy

CONTACT
760.749.3333
www.batesfarm.com

California's diverse landscapes offer many ideal settings in which to explore and relax after only a short drive. Such is the case with the Bates Nut Farm tour. Only an hour from San Diego, visitors can relax and enjoy an afternoon on a picturesque farm.

The Bates Nut Farm is full of nuts, but that isn't what the tour is about. On this self-guided tour, visitors have a chance to escape to the country.

Pulling into the driveway, the country life greets you immediately. The large open pens of farm animals are right next to the parking lot. From small goats to loud chickens, the children will love how close they can get. The animals seem to love it too, as they step close to the fence with seemingly equal curiosity. Visitors are able to walk around and explore the nut-producing trees and grounds at their leisure.

The outhouse right outside the store is a reminder that the "good old days" were sometimes a bit rough, especially when it came time to take care of life's basic necessities.

Inside the store at Bates Nut Farm, visitors will get the chance to see how many different nut products are produced here. From jumbo pecans to California Pistachios, the opportunity to find out more about nut production is an interesting part of this tour. Samples are offered throughout the store and the farm has several picnic tables for eating lunch.

TAKE THE TOUR

WHERE TO GO
30841 Cole Grade Road
Valley Center, CA 92082

WHEN TO GO
Self-Guided Tours
10am – 4pm daily

DEGREE OF DIFFICULTY
Easy

CONTACT
760.749.6297
www.bellgardensfarm.com

BELL GARDENS

Only an hour from San Diego, this is a self-guided tour of a working farm. Depending on the time of year, visitors can see what a working farm looks like, from plowing and planting to harvesting.

The founder of Bell Gardens, Glen W. Bell Jr., is the founder of the Taco Bell fast food chain. He so loved growing up on a farm and working outdoors that he wanted to share this affection with others by creating a park-like setting in which to share his experience. Bell's love for the farm is contagious because all the people who work here treat the guests with the same enthusiasm.

When visitors arrive at the gardens, a pen of geese greets them. Next to the geese is the famous bell used in the Taco Bell logo. The best place to begin the tour is at the demonstration gardens. Here visitors get the chance to see how different crops are raised. From the ordinary to the absolutely extraordinary, this is one of the best demonstration gardens you will find. There are cotton plants, strawberry patches, squash and many other vegetables marked for easy identification. Picnic tables under the nearby trees are available for lunch or just a break.

From the picnic area, it is a short walk down the hill to check out the different farming equipment. Several tractors are available for a close up look and a picture for anyone who wants to look like a farmer. Farther afield are Mr. Bell's berry and pumpkin patches.

Since this is a working farm, everything grown here is available for purchase in the open-air country store. A free walking map of the farm is available in the store outlining the fields and what is planted in them. Because there is no hurry in the country, visitors are welcome to stay as long as they wish.

BUENA VISTA AUDUBON NATURE CENTER

Whether you love birds or simply want to learn more about them, a visit to the Buena Vista Audubon Nature Center in Oceanside is a must for any vacation. This nature center is located next to the Buena Vista Lagoon and is one of the best opportunities to see many birds that call California home. The tours start at the nature center, which is on the North side of the property.

Greeting visitors in the parking lot is a steel sculpture of a bird. Inside the building, a small exhibition hall displays stuffed birds, bird nests and other items relating to birds and bird watching. Especially exciting is the exhibit of bird's eggs. From tiny hummingbird eggs to giant ostrich eggs, the colors and shapes are fascinating. Knowing that the eggs we get from the grocery store are uniform, this display demonstrates what eggs in the wild are like. The interactive exhibits available include touching eggs, feathers and nests. Fragile and small, the chance to touch these items is worth the visit alone.

Outside the nature center visitors can learn the finer points of bird watching. Birds can be heard singing and seen swooping through the skies above and nesting around the nearby lagoon. Additionally, there are displays that give information about the birds and the lagoon. While visitors are limited in how far they can go into the lagoon area, there is no need to worry about missing out, an endless variety of birds fly around the nature center.

While the displays and kiosks are interesting, the real value of this tour is the enthusiastic and insightful information provided by the docents who work at the facility. Energetic and full of facts, the docents take time to get involved with visitors - be they adults or a third grade class - and are happy to answer questions and give tours. Each month the Buena Vista Audubon Nature Center provides classes and informative lectures on various bird-related topics. Call the center for more information on these opportunities.

TAKE THE TOUR

WHERE TO GO
2202 South Coast Highway
Oceanside, CA 92049

WHEN TO GO
Self-Guided Tours
Tuesday - Saturday
10am - 4pm
Sunday 1pm - 4pm
Guided Tours
Reservations Required

DEGREE OF DIFFICULTY
Easy

CONTACT
760.439.2473

CALIFORNIA SURF MUSEUM

Only blocks from the ocean, the California Surf Museum pays tribute to those who live to hang ten. Just mention the sandy beaches of Southern California and you immediately form a picture of palm trees, convertible cars and surfers. For visitors who surf, this tour is a must.

When most people think of surfing they think it all began in the 60s with the Beach Boys and Frankie Avalon and Annette Funicello singing and dancing in the sand. However, the first mention of riding waves while standing on a length of wood can be traced back to the mid-1700s when written accounts by explorer Captain James Cook and his crew described men riding on the surf with crude boards.

When the sport was still in its modern infancy in the 1950's, teens that didn't have money for a board would make do with their mothers' ironing board. The shape, weight, and composition of a surfboard allow surfers to ride different types and sizes of waves.

In addition to the California surf experience, a major focus of the museum is on Hawaiian surfing. Paying tribute to Duke Kahanamoku, known worldwide as the father of modern surfing, visitors will gain an appreciation for his impact on the sport. The displays of Hawaiian olo boards (from 12 to 22 feet long) used only by royalty are display along with shorter alaia boards (6 to 12 feet long) used by Hawaiian commoners.

The boards on display show how the sport has evolved through the years. From solid wood to lighter fiberglass, boards are more portable and maneuverable today. While the sport and its equipment has changed over the past 250 years, the waves and people's desire to ride them, remain the same.

CALLAWAY GOLF BALLS

While the white, dimpled balls that fly through the air at your local golf course look simple enough, the process to make them perfect is much more complicated. The shape, weight and spin of these small balls can make or break a golfer's game. The guided tour at the Callaway Golf Company is a fascinating one for golf enthusiasts or anyone interested in the amazing world of precision craftsmanship.

Callaway Golf has been making golf clubs and equipment for more than 20 years. Their products are used by some of the best golfers in the world, including Arnold Palmer. But while they have built their business around golf clubs, their expansion into making golf balls is just over a year old. The quality of their balls is excellent and they are now the third most popular golf ball in the United States.

TAKE THE TOUR
WHERE TO GO 2180 Rutherford Road Carlsbad, CA 92008
WHEN TO GO *Guided Tours* Reservations Required
DEGREE OF DIFFICULTY Easy
CONTACT 760.930.8687 **www.callawaygolf.com**

The factory tour lasts roughly an hour and provides a look at the precision machinery used to make these popular golf balls. Before visitors can begin the tour, everyone must sign a nondisclosure agreement to protect Callaway's trade secrets.

The creation of the ball core is the first stop on the tour. The core material is mixed in a large machine and the individual cores are rounded in a process that ensures that they are perfect spheres. Once the core is made, the white, dimpled ball cover is applied. The unique, aerodynamic dimples are designed to ensure the ball flies straight, if hit straight, of course. The balls are then coated with a clear paint and imprinted with the Callaway name. From there, the golf balls are inspected for quality and stored in 55-gallon drums to await packaging.

The tour ends with the logo imprint line of balls. These are the special golf balls sold exclusively with the logos of tournaments or other special events. In this room the golf balls are imprinted with a company's logo for promotional purposes. The technology used in this process is extraordinary and so is the collection of all the golf balls that Callaway has imprinted. More than 400 custom imprinted balls are on display.

CALLAWAY GOLF CLUBS

TAKE THE TOUR

WHERE TO GO
2180 Rutherford Road
Carlsbad, CA 92008

WHEN TO GO
Guided Tours
Reservations Required

DEGREE OF DIFFICULTY
Easy

CONTACT
760.930.8687
www.callawaygolf.com

Care and attention are necessary to select a good golf club long before it is given a trial swing at the shop. The Callaway Golf tour is an opportunity to see how clubs are manufactured with the optimum balance to produce the best possible control. Callaway Golf has become famous for its putters, irons and especially its Big Bertha woods, all of which are made in Carlsbad, California. Distributed nationally and internationally, Callaway has become synonymous with quality in the golf industry.

Before starting the tour, all visitors are required to sign a nondisclosure agreement to protect trade secrets. This takes a few minutes so it is important to arrive a little early to not miss the tour. Headphones are supplied to make it easier to hear what the guide is saying during the tour. This is especially helpful in the factory, which is fairly noisy. During the tour, visitors are required to stay within the lines painted on the floor - close enough to see what is going on, yet far enough away for safety.

There are two parts to a club: the shaft and the head. Connecting these two parts is more difficult than it might seem and the tour explains how precisely these two pieces must fit and stay together. Any problems with mounting the shaft to the head can lead to the wood in the head splitting from the impact of hitting the ball

or, in the case of metal clubs, undesirable vibration.

Assembling a club is an art that involves lasers for measuring and aligning the two pieces. Especially interesting is how each club is weighed to make them exactly the same. The weights are inserted by hand and machine with such care that they are invisible to the naked eye. Once a club is assembled, the next step is polishing and cleaning. To ensure the club is perfect, quality control is continuously stressed throughout the production process. The last part of the tour is packaging. Each club is bagged, coded and inventoried; placed in a box and shipped to customers around the world. Callaway golf clubs are coded to indicate what day they were made and where they were sold.

Another interesting part of the tour is the custom line where specialized golf clubs are made. Custom clubs are only available by special order. Using some of the same equipment found on the factory line, the craftsman in the custom center build a single club from start to finish instead of focusing on one part of the process.

TAKE THE TOUR

WHERE TO GO
8860 Lawrence Welk Drive
Escondido, CA 92026

WHEN TO GO
Self-Guided Tour
9am - 4:45pm Daily

DEGREE OF DIFFICULTY
Easy

CONTACT
760.749.3448
www.welkresort.com

LAWRENCE WELK MUSEUM

The Lawrence Welk Show was one of the most popular prime time shows of the 1960's. A variety show on ABC, Welk brought music and laughter into homes across America. Today the memories and nostalgia behind this popular man reside at the Lawrence Welk Museum. The museum rests on the Lawrence Welk Resort Community just outside of Escondido on Highway 15. Past the big sign, in the small shopping village, just before the living community is an opportunity to learn about this talented individual.

Visitors are greeted by a replica of the television show's bandstand. A full sized ABC camera, once used to film the show stands off to the left of the bandstand. This is a great place for photographs, especially for anyone who ever wanted to sing or dance on the show but missed the opportunity. The music chairs and music music stands have a certain distinction. Also inside the door is the chandelier given to Mr. Welk for his 25th Anniversary show. This huge fixture gives an idea of how successful the show was.

To the right of the doors hangs an oversized portrait of Lawrence Welk. Taking the upper half of an entire wall, visitors can't help but feel very close to the star. Further along on the left, pictures also highlight popular scenes from the show. From the first production to the different celebrities who visited, this is a trip down memory lane.

For those who forget how Lawrence got started, one of the accordions he played during the early years of his career is on display. In mint condition, the instrument gives a perspective on how someone who played a simple accordion got to be an international superstar.

Another wonderful exhibit is the radio studio reconstructed to look like the first one Mr. Welk played in. The microphone is the size of two fists and really gives some perspective on how much entertainment technology has changed.

For those who have never seen The Lawrence Welk Show or haven't for a few or ten years, it is a good idea to catch an episode before the tour. This will make the experience all the more memorable.

NATIONAL RV FACTORY TOUR

TAKE THE TOUR

WHERE TO GO
3411 Perris Blvd
Perris, CA 92571

WHEN TO GO
Guided Tours
Monday - Friday 3pm

DEGREE OF DIFFICULTY
Moderate

CONTACT
909.943.6007
www.nrvh.com/national/
company/tour

National RV is one of the top manufacturers of recreational vehicles in the country. They produce two types of vehicles: travel trailers that are pulled behind cars or trucks and motorhomes.

The tour covers how National RV builds its motorhomes at the facility in Perris, California. The tour takes about two hours and covers the entire production process, from building the chassis to the final paint job.

Starting with the chassis, the base of the motorhome is the first priority. Making sure the wires and plumbing are in their proper places, the tour moves along to show how the sides are fastened together. As the vehicle takes shape moving along the production line, a crew is working on the interior to make sure when it rolls off the line the entire vehicle is finished.

The tour includes not just how the vehicle is constructed, but also how the cabinets and systems inside the vehicle are made and placed into the final product. Craftsmen who work only a few steps away from the assembly line make most of the interior.

Quality control at this plant is a high priority. Ensuring the vehicle is ready for the consumer, the unit must pass rigorous testing on all moving parts before it is allowed off the property.

ORFILA VINEYARDS

TAKE THE TOUR

WHERE TO GO
13455 San Pasquel Road
Escondido, CA 92025

WHEN TO GO
Self-Guided Tours
10am – 6pm Daily
Guided Tours
2 p.m. Daily

DEGREE OF DIFFICULTY
Easy

CONTACT
760.738.6500
www.orfila.com

An uncommon enthusiasm for wine making coupled with the desire to share that enthusiasm with visitors, makes the Orfila Vineyards tour special. Visitors can walk around and explore wine making on a self guided tour that is outlined by numbered stations on a free handout.

At the first stop, visitors are invited outside to view the vineyard. Only steps from the winery, the neatly kept rows line the hillside as far as the eye can see. In late August or early September the harvesting begins as employees pick grapes by hand. Rose bushes planted on the ends of the rows of grape vines are not only there to make the area pretty. These roses help monitor the vineyards by showing signs of disease, mildew, pests and other problems before the grape plants do.

Back towards the winery is the receiving area for harvested grapes. The grapes are deposited by a rotating forklift into a hopper. A machine then removes any remaining stems and the grapes are put in a press where they are crushed by hand. This traditional, hand crafted technique is also used in Burgundy, France.

Once the grapes are pressed, the juice is pumped into temperature controlled steel tanks. Yeast is added to start the fermentation process before the wine is moved into barrels. The aisle of oak barrels is where the fermenting red wine is stored for aging. The wood allows the wine to breathe during this process, reducing bitter flavors while also adding spice and toasty oak flavors to the wine.

Once the wine has aged, it ends up at the bottling line. The bottling is done in four stages. Glass bottles move down a conveyor belt and are filled. A cork is inserted into the neck of the bottle while another machine affixes a capsule to the neck. Finally, a label is placed on the bottle and it is loaded into a carton.

The tour ends in the tasting room where visitors of age can sample Orfila's wine and purchase a bottle or other tasteful gifts.

TAYLOR MADE GOLF CLUBS

TAKE THE TOUR

WHERE TO GO
5545 Fermi Court
Carlsbad, CA 92008

WHEN TO GO
Guided Tours
Reservations Required

DEGREE OF DIFFICULTY
Moderate

CONTACT
760.918.6000
www.taylormadegolf.com

Those who golf yearn to feel the swing of a perfect club. When a smooth swing connects squarely with a ball, the feeling is amazing. Just as amazing is the process of creating those perfect clubs and the tour at Taylor Made Golf Clubs is a great opportunity to see this process first hand.

Driving to the facility, visitors pass a golf course situated next to the main building. Before the tour begins, visitors are required to sign a release form that protects the trade secrets that are shared on the tour, so it's no surprise that cameras and recorders are not allowed in the facility.

The tour begins with the production line. Boxes of heads, shafts and grips are lined up waiting to be assembled into clubs. The assembly line is focused on creating a quality product while paying attention to details. The head, shaft and grip are joined in a simple process by precision equipment.

Once assembled, the club is weighed and to ensure that it is balanced. An electronic scale is used to measure each club. If the weight is off by even a fraction of an ounce, small weights are placed

THE MOST INTERESTING PART OF THE TAYLOR MADE TOUR IS THE RESEARCH FACILITY

inside the head. These weights are so small and integrated into the head with such skill that unless they are pointed out, you would never notice them. After the club is weighed, it is polished and checked for quality. If the club meets Taylor's stringent standards, it is wrapped and placed in packaging for shipment to golf shops and sporting goods stores.

The most interesting part of the Taylor Made tour is the research facility. Continually striving to improve their products, Taylor Made has a laboratory for developing materials, forms and manufacturing methods that lead to better clubs. In their lab, the guide will point out machines that test the golf clubs. Striking hundreds of golf balls with the clubs, the researchers determine how many strokes can be taken before their golf clubs no longer function correctly.

The professional building shop is the final stop on the tour. Here, custom clubs ordered by professional golfers are hand made to exact specifications.

While Taylor Made only manufactures clubs for United States golfing standards at this facility, they have another plant in Asia that makes brightly painted and decorated clubs for the individual taste of the golfer. But despite their odd looks, the clubs play with the same precision as all of Taylor's clubs.

TAKE THE TOUR

WHERE TO GO
32605 Holland Road
Winchester CA 92596

WHEN TO GO
Self-Guided Tours
Guided Tours
Monday – Friday
9am - 5pm
Saturday – Sunday
10am – 4pm
Reservations Required

DEGREE OF DIFFICULTY
Easy
Contact
909.926.4239
www.winchestercheese.com

WINCHESTER CHEESE

A short drive to the country will give visitors the opportunity to see how some of California's best cheese is made. On this short walking tour the entire process, from milk to Gouda, is explained in tasty detail. Following a European family tradition, the cheese is made from recipes handed down over generations.

At this working farm, visitors are greeted by a pen of animals. From a couple of calves to a pig, the farm animals are another enjoyable part of the tour. The majority of the milk cows can be found just behind the main building. Cows and calves live on the farm with a few bulls to watch the herd. Looking carefully, visitors might get the chance to see a calf. The calves are by far the most entertaining of the farm animals as they run circles around their mothers.

To begin the tour, walk around the front of the building and take the stairs up to the window for a view into the making of Gouda. In a large vat, milk is mixed with bacteria culture and other ingredients. Curds are allowed to form and the leftover liquid is poured off. Once the curds are formed, they are packed into round containers to set. Once the curds form together, the next concern is to keep the cheese's flavor intact. The outside, darker orange part of the cheese is an edible vegetable sealing wax that is brushed on the side of the cheese. This creates a seal that keeps flavor in and air out. Great tasting cheese is important at Winchester, as evidenced by the continuous quality control practiced here. The cheese makers mark down all the variations in a batch daily to ensure they produce the best possible cheese.

The cheese is then aged in walk-in refrigerators that are stacked with shelves of wheel after wheel of Gouda. Small signs with the date and type hang from the racks allowing the cheese makers to track their inventory. Once the cheese has aged enough to develop the best taste, it is cut and sealed for distribution.

After finishing the tour, visitors are invited to enjoy samples. Four different flavors of Gouda are available, offering a tasty end to this tour.

Tours *FOR* **FREE**™

ARCO OLYMPIC CENTER

BALBOA PARK

BERNARDO WINERY

BUCK KNIVES

HOTEL DEL CORONADO

MUSEUM OF CONTEMPORARY
ART DOWNTOWN

OLD TOWN SAN DIEGO
STATE HISTORICAL PARK

SALK INSTITUTE FOR
BIOLOGICAL STUDIES

SAN DIEGO MINERAL
AND GEM SOCIETY

SAN DIEGO UNION TRIBUNE

SUMMERS PAST FARMS

TAYLOR GUITARS

THE TIMKEN MUSEUM OF ART

WELLS FARGO HISTORY MUSEUM

SAN DIEGO

ARCO OLYMPIC CENTER

United States Olympic athletes don't become world champions by chance; they train for months, if not years, under strict supervision. The tour of the Arco Olympic Training Center takes visitors behind the scenes and into the daily life of Olympic hopefuls at this one of three U.S. Olympic Training Centers.

The athletes who participate in Olympic games put in serious time and effort in their quest for gold. They spend several hours each day training in their sport, cross training to build up muscles and endurance, all while following strict diets. All of this is done under the direction of their coaches. The Olympic center provides all this to its athletes, at no cost, for their exclusive use.

The tour starts inside the visitor center and after a brief overview of the athletes who use the facility; visitors spend the next hour seeing just what life as an Olympic athlete is like.

The first stop is the professional soccer fields. The Olympic Center is meticulous about its facilities and that is reflected in the perfect turf, maintained to prevent injuries. Other views along the way include the softball fields where the Gold Medal U.S. Women's Softball team practices, the bike path which crosses under the

TAKE THE TOUR

WHERE TO GO
2800 Olympic Parkway
Chula Vista, CA 91915

WHEN TO GO
Self-Guided Tours and
Guided tours
Monday - Friday
10am - 4pm
Saturday 9am - 4pm
Sunday 11am - 4pm
Guided Tours
On the hour

DEGREE OF DIFFICULTY
Moderate

CONTACT
619.656.1500
www.usolympicteam.com

Olympic Pathway where Olympic hopefuls train and the archery range.

The Olympic Center in Chula Vista is the main training site for the U.S. Olympic Archery Team. The outside fields provide an unmatched practice range. During the tour, visitors can watch target practice in a sport that demands concentration, perfect breath control and patience.

The personal facilities for the athletes are large buildings on the East side of the Olympic Pathway. Here they eat, sleep and work out in a specially designed indoor gym. The life of the athletes in this secluded area is intended to ensure that they stay focused on their training.

In addition to the guided tour, the Olympic Center is available for self-guided tours and the beautifully manicured grounds are a sight to see. The center has useful signage to guide visitors along the pathway. The downside of the self-guided tour is that visitors don't get the benefit of asking questions of the knowledgeable volunteer guides. The insights and stories shared by the tour guides are worth the visit itself.

BALBOA PARK

TAKE THE TOUR

WHERE TO GO
1549 El Prado
San Diego, CA 92101

WHEN TO GO
Self Guided Tours
9am - 4pm daily

DEGREE OF DIFFICULTY
Moderate

CONTACT
619.239.0512
www.balboapark.org

Going to Balboa Park in San Diego is like stepping into another world. The park, opened in the early 1900's, is home to thousands of plants and exotic flowers. More than just a huge park, with every turn visitors will find themselves immersed in a new culture through the international themes that make this a great place to see.

The actual park is laid out in small complexes, divided by streets that are primarily limited to use by pedestrians. The layout makes it easy to get around, and the best free thing to do is simply walk around the grounds. From the Spanish style décor of the El Prado Building to the bell tower standing in the middle of the park, visitors begin to experience the fusion of Spanish and Western Culture. Standing in the spray from the fountains in the center of the park and in front of the Museum of Natural History is a great way to cool off on a hot day.

One highlight of the tour is the old fig tree next to the Museum of Natural History. While you are not able to touch the trunk or run underneath, the size alone is truly amazing. The tree's canopy covers half a city block and fills the air with leaves.

Visitors interested in the arts will enjoy the Spanish Art Village. Within the village, more than 20 artisans have set up shop and give demonstrations of their art. From glass blowing to pottery, visitors can see something different everyday.

For those interested in a world-class art museum, a visit to the Timken is in order (See the Timken Tour on page 137).

BUCK KNIVES

A good sharp knife is standard equipment for anyone who spends time outdoors. From slicing fruit to building an emergency shelter, these tools are indispensable. The Buck family has created a brand synonymous with quality and craftsmanship. This tour gives visitors a chance to see how

Buck Knives makes its various styles from eight-inch hunting knives to pocket pen knives. From the creation of the blades to the process used to connect the handles, this tour covers the entire, fascinating process of knife making. Because most of the process involves working with metal, visitors are required to wear safety glasses throughout the tour.

The most important part of a knife is the blade and the tour begins with the raw metal sheets used for making them. There are two methods for creating knife blades from metal. Smaller blades are die cut from a roll of metal streaming through a machine while larger blades are cut from thicker metal sheets by a computer-controlled laser cutter. The width of the knife blade determines which process is used.

The shape of the blade is the focus at the beginning of the process; the edge comes later. Next to the laser cutting machine are samples of the several different knives produced.

Once the blades are cut, they are tumbled in a fine abrasive to remove any jagged edges that could cut employees during the assembly process. After tumbling, the blades are checked for strength and structure before being sent to the assembly line where the blades are sorted by size and sent to get handles. The simple, one-piece knives used for hunting usually have a specialized handle that is attached without further work being done on the blade. Depending on the size of the knife, the process varies. Basically the handle for a hunting knife is made of two parts, snapped together by a machine powered by an air compressor. The smaller, folding pocketknives are usually assembled with several accessories, such as a fingernail file or screwdriver, in addition to the covering on each side of the knife. The parts are assembled by hand with small metal posts that are the pivot point for the blade and accessories. Once aligned, the blade and accessories are pressed together with an air compressor.

Each part of the knife is polished by hand and then the blade is sharpened. A craftsman uses a grinding wheel to put a uniform edge on the blade. After this is done, the knife is polished again and checked in the quality control area for any defects. The tour ends at the gift shop where visitors can see the wide variety of styles made by Buck Knives.

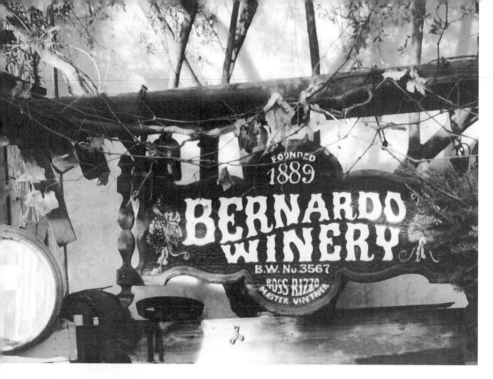

TAKE THE TOUR

WHERE TO GO
13330 Paseo Del Verano Norte
San Diego, CA 92128

WHEN TO GO
Self Guided Tours
9am - 5pm Daily

DEGREE OF DIFFICULTY
Easy

CONTACT
858.487.1866
www.bernardowinery.com

BERNARDO WINERY

One of the oldest operating vineyards and wineries in the San Diego region, Bernardo Winery is a great place to take an afternoon drive and explore. Established in 1889, the winery retains a sense of the old wine country before subdivisions were developed around the vineyard.

Arranged into a small village, it is a cinch for visitors to find their way around once they find the center of the complex – the winery store. After picking up the map for the tour, it is time to start exploring. The wine is made right in front of the store. A building just to the right usually is open for visitors to step in and look. Large steel containers full of wine are in this room. Blending the working winery with life, there are plenty of interesting knickknacks that hang on the walls. Take a minute to absorb the smell and ambiance of this interesting room.

Just outside the building and around the corner there is a display of old fashioned farming equipment. The majority of this equipment was actually used at the winery. This is a great spot to take a few snapshots so bring the camera.

Left of the store is a small vineyard. Here grape vines soak up the sun in preparation for the next the harvest and next line of delicious wine. A stroll through the vineyard is a must for any winery tour.

The remainder of the village is full of interesting and varied shops to explore. From the outdoor glass blower to a framing studio, visitors will want to look around before heading back to the winery for samples of wine.

HOTEL DEL CORONADO

TAKE THE TOUR

WHERE TO GO
1500 Orange Avenue
Coronado, CA 92118

WHEN TO GO
Self-Guided Tour
10am-9pm Daily

DEGREE OF DIFFICULTY
Easy

CONTACT
619.435.6611
www.hoteldel.com

Located on Coronado Island, this beautiful hotel and its colorful history are just waiting to be discovered. The tour is self-guided and is a chance to get acquainted with this national historic landmark and to enjoy the beauty of the island at your own pace.

The most widely recognized building, the Hotel del Coronado, was completed in early 1888 and opened its doors to the public on February 19th of that year. At the time, this building was the largest structure outside of New York City to be lighted with electricity and Thomas Edison, the inventor of the light bulb, personally supervised the installation of his bright lights. A popular summer vacation destination, the Coronado was known for its famous guests. The impressive guest list includes Marilyn Monroe, Ronald Reagan and L. Frank Baum, author of the Wizard Of Oz.

The picturesque front of the hotel is a popular photo opportunity and its red roofs and white stucco Spanish architecture is beautiful at sunset.

The main floor is covered with lush carpet that whispers elegance with every step. Just past the registration desk is the library with tile walls covered with a myriad of relics and historic knick-knacks and photos. Don't be surprised if you bump into Kate Morgan, the famous ghost from room 3312 who is said to wander the hotel looking for her husband. She checked in November, 1892 and never checked out.

After soaking up this area, press on and take the old fashioned elevator to the basement which is filled with stores and an opportunity for a little shopping. Visitors can walk through this area and weave their way outside to the back of the hotel where a walkway winds through the beautiful grounds to the beach. This beach offers some of the best places to find starfish, crabs and snails living among tidal pools.

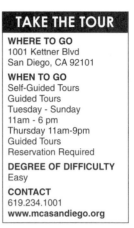

TAKE THE TOUR

WHERE TO GO
1001 Kettner Blvd
San Diego, CA 92101

WHEN TO GO
Self-Guided Tours
Guided Tours
Tuesday - Sunday
11am - 6 pm
Thursday 11am-9pm
Guided Tours
Reservation Required

DEGREE OF DIFFICULTY
Easy

CONTACT
619.234.1001
www.mcasandiego.org

MUSEUM OF CONTEMPORARY ART

In the center of San Diego, visitors can find a place to hide from the hustle and bustle of the city and quietly enjoy the eclectic sights of contemporary art. A branch of the Museum of Contemporary Art in La Jolla, this gallery leans toward more modern art and the displays change often.

The tour starts on the main floor in a large room full of exhibits. The volunteer tour guides take time to talk about the art and the artist, which adds much to the experience. In a smaller adjoining room, more pieces are on display.

Upstairs there are exhibits from different artists and, again, guides are on hand to answer questions and discuss the work being shown. Also on this floor is a scale model of the new location the MCA hopes to open in the next couple of years.

Before leaving, don't forget to check out the 20-foot tall moving metal cut-out sculpture of a man swinging a hammer.

OLD TOWN SAN DIEGO STATE HISTORICAL PARK

TAKE THE TOUR

WHERE TO GO
4002 Wallace Street
San Diego, CA 92110

WHEN TO GO
Guided Tours
11am & 2 pm Daily

DEGREE OF DIFFICULTY
Easy

CONTACT
619.220.5422
www.sandiegohistory.org/
links/oldtown.htm

Old Town is a chance for visitors to get a feel for what San Diego was like before California was a state. Old Town was designated a state historic park in 1968 and there is on going restoration of the original adobes and other buildings around the plaza, including Seeley Stable.

Guides dressed in period attire give tours of Old Town that last about an hour. They do a good job relating the history and significance of the buildings as well as providing fun facts about the park. The tour is worthwhile because the information provided by the guides can not be found walking around or reading the plaques and historic markers.

The tour begins at the Robinson–Rose House, a building that was the commercial center of this time period and the current location of the visitor center. It housed the offices of James Robinson, a successful businessman and attorney, the Sand Diego Herald, the railroad and other private stores and offices. Next stop in the plaza is the flag pole, assumed to be an old ship's main mast and the location of the first American flag raised here on July 29, 1846 by a detachment of Marines from the U.S. Navy Sloop, Cyane.

The tour moves from building to building, including a stop in the Seeley Stable. This building was headquarters for the Concord stages in the San Diego-Los Angeles Stage Line. The coaches would make the 130-mile trip in less than 24 hours. However, that all changed when the railroad arrived and put Albert Seeley out of business.

The San Diego Union Building is another fascinating building. The wooden building was actually built in Maine and shipped around Cape Horn in 1851. It was

the first home of the city's newspaper and its well-preserved interior give visitors a chance to see what a newsroom of the day looked like. The Washington hand press on display is the same type used to print the first edition. Visitors to the San Diego Union-Tribune tour (page 133) will notice a significant difference in the way the paper is produced today. These two tours together offer a great comparison to show how technology has changed the way we live.

Winding around, don't forget to stop at the San Diego Courthouse, the first fired-brick structure in the area. The School Building, built in 1865, was one of the first schoolhouses in San Diego. Mary Chase Walker, the first teacher, was paid $65 a month to teach the children. The tour of Old Town not only offers a captivating look at how early Californians lived in San Diego, but also provides a quality presentation from the guides and the well tended grounds.

SALK INSTITUTE OF BIOLOGICAL STUDIES

The Salk Institute is named for Jonas Salk who developed the Polio vaccine. This tour not only highlights the innovative science taking place at the complex, but the compelling structures that make this facility famous as well. The Salk Institute was founded in 1960 on land given to the city. The mission of the institute is to discover the origins and structure of diseases such as cancer, AIDS, Alzheimers, Parkinson's, diabetes and birth defects – not to search for cures.

The 26-acre campus overlooks the Pacific Ocean from the Torrey Pines Mesa in La Jolla. Marrying art and medicine, architect Louis Kahn and Jonas Salk collaborated on designing the campus. Mindful about the continuous changes in science and research methods, the two designed laboratory spaces that could be adapted for different uses and equipment while making use of the abundant natural light.

The tour takes about an hour and is guided by a volunteer, who does a good job explaining the architectural importance of these buildings in their own right as well as the world renowned research occurring inside. The guide points out the shapes such as triangles, squares, and circles in the architecture in locations easily overlooked in a quick passing.

The combination of the two identical main buildings with pine forested surroundings seems to hide the fact that the buildings are six stories tall. Three main floors house laboratories while three lesser floors house equipment. In the center, a grand courtyard of travertine marble acts as a pretense to the sky with the ocean in the background.

The buildings are made out a pink-hued concrete similar to that used by the Romans. The poured-in-place concrete walls have been left unfinished to provide a simple, unassuming look. Another great feature of the design is that all faculty members have offices facing the ocean.

In addition to the older structures, a new East building was built to help with the growth of the facility. Similar in design to the original buildings, the new structure contains a 300-seat auditorium directly under a pedestrian walkway.

Enjoying the thoughtful and pleasing design of the architecture at the Salk Institute, it's easy to forget about the important research going on inside. However, the comfortable surroundings help the scientist focus on their work, and make the Salk tour a must see for anyone traveling or living in the area.

TAKE THE TOUR

WHERE TO GO
10010 N. Torrey Pines Rd.
La Jolla, CA 92037

WHEN TO GO
Guided Tours
Reservations required

DEGREE OF DIFFICULTY
Moderate

CONTACT
858.453.4100
www.salk.edu

TAKE THE TOUR

WHERE TO GO
1700 Village Place
Balboa Park
San Diego, CA 92101

WHEN TO GO
Self Guided Tours
11am - 4pm Daily

DEGREE OF DIFFICULTY
Easy

CONTACT
619.239.8812

SAN DIEGO MINERAL AND GEM SOCIETY

Located in the Spanish Artist complex in Balboa Park, this tour is an interesting look into the origins of a variety of gems and minerals, from diamonds to geodes. The exhibits offer excellent and concise information on how minerals and gems are formed, their properties, and what makes some more valuable than others. Even the most novice of rock and fossil hounds will find this tour captivating.

Right inside the door is probably one of the most fascinating items in Balboa Park – a fossilized whale bone the size of a large desk. The walls around the room hold displays on various minerals and gems, including fabulous specimens. Closer to the exit visitors can see a real diamond cutter at work and a display gives step-by-step instructions on how the diamond cutter is used. The information center is a great resource for anyone interested in starting a rock or mineral collection of their own.

SAN DIEGO UNION-TRIBUNE

The original site of the San Diego Union is found at the San Diego's Old Town State Historic Park. Started in 1868, the paper was printed on a hand press and was four pages long. The paper became the San Diego Union-Tribune when the morning and afternoon editions merged after the newspapers were purchased by the Copley News Service. Today, the daily newspaper is the 20th largest in the country and the second largest in California.

The tour covers the basics of the editorial process and the daily production of the newspaper. Both are housed at this facility in two separate buildings. The two are separate due to the incredible noise of the presses; no one could get their work done with all that racket.

The tour starts in the lobby where a collection of vintage presses once used to print the paper are on display. These are an introduction to the modern newsroom that awaits upstairs. A sea of desks, separated by partial walls, is where reporters work. Some of the stories they report come from news tips, police activity and even the fax machine which, when you walk by on the tour will more than likely be spewing pages of press releases. The newsroom is divided into sections, just as the paper itself is divided into different sections, from local news, sports, and features to business.

The photography section of the newspaper works very closely with the reporters and editors to provide images to help tell the stories. Other people in this area produce graphics and design elements for the paper, such as maps, illustrations and creative layouts. The next part of the tour is in the second building, accessed via a walkway, where the presses are located. These machines are so loud that they need their own building with no windows.

Once the stories are edited and ready to print, they are electronically sent to the production facility where the stories are combined with the ads, photos and other graphic elements. The page is transferred to a plate (a metal sheet with a negative image of the page) which are then attached to the presses. Each plate on a color page prints a different primary color on a particular page. These colors overlap perfectly so that the different hues combine to create a sharp, clear image on the printed page.

Looking through windows, visitors can watch the four Goss Metro Presses in action. The newsprint moves through the rollers picking up the different color inks to make the images we see on the newspaper. Once the printing is completed, the paper is folded and prepared to be inserted. The final stop on the tour are the big machines that insert the advertisements into the paper. Using compressed air, the machines collate the advertisements and insert them in the paper. This entire process takes place at amazing speeds to ensure that the papers are delivered on time.

SUMMERS PAST FARMS

Just outside San Diego is a remarkable farm called the Summers Past Farms. Located on Old Highway 80, this tranquil and educational tour should be on everyone's list. From the moment visitors arrive in the parking lot, they are greeted by the rich smells of the crops growing in the fields. Depending on the season, the colors and smells may vary, but no matter what the time of year there are many wonders throughout the farm.

A walk in the garden is an enchanting experience. A small pathway winds around the first picture perfect garden through which a small stream flows. There are several small benches along the way to stop and enjoy the songs of birds in the nearby trees. After walking a little further past the stream, visitors come upon a vegetable and flower garden.

The kid's garden, just behind the main building, is a place where children can get their hands dirty and learn what gardening is all about. With the emphasis on fun, the garden is a miniature replica of the adult garden.

The soap and gardening shop are open for visitors and in between the two shops are plants offered for sale and a small outdoor soda stand. As the name implies, Summers Past Farm is a laid back tour and a great escape from the hectic pace of modern living.

TAKE THE TOUR

WHERE TO GO
1980 Gillespie Way
El Cajon, CA 92020

WHEN TO GO
Guided Tours
Monday - Friday 1pm

DEGREE OF DIFFICULTY
Easy

CONTACT
619.258.6957
www.taylorguitars.com

TAYLOR GUITARS

Everyone would agree that there is an art to making music, but not everyone thinks about the art of making the instruments that make music possible. The Taylor Guitar tour is a chance to see first hand the art of producing these finely crafted instruments. The guitars made at this facility include the traditional Series Taylor, Baby Taylor and guitars in the Acoustic Bass series.

The tour starts in the back of the building with the beginnings of a guitar. Looking at rough sheets of fine wood, visitors are introduced to a guitar in its most basic stage. Specially selected types of wood, from Sapele to Indian Rosewood, create their own unique sound or pitch in the instrument. The moisture content of the wood is also important and should be around 18 percent to achieve the best quality sound.

One of the beauties of a guitar is the uniformity of the wood grain. Upon close inspection, the same patterns are found throughout a well-made guitar, even if the wood was glued together from multiple pieces. The next part of the tour reveals the presses used to make these patterns. After the wood is taken out of the presses, lasers are used to cut the pattern that will become the top and the bottom of the body of the guitar.

To make the curving sides a mold apparatus is used to shape strips of wood. The neck of the guitar is next and it, too, is cut from carefully selected wood by lasers. After the wood pieces and machinery are assembled, they are placed on a rack and sprayed with a clear coat of varnish. Finally, the instrument is strung and ready for a quality control audition and final touches. The tour ends in the small museum room full of company memorabilia.

The instruments made by Taylor Guitars are far from ordinary. Some have inlayed coral on the necks while others are painstakingly made by hand for famous musicians. Fascinating and informative, this tour is for the serious musician as well as anyone who loves music.

THE TIMKEN MUSEUM OF ART

TAKE THE TOUR

WHERE TO GO
1500 El Prado
Balboa Park
San Diego, CA 92101

WHEN TO GO
Self-Guided Tours
Tuesday – Saturday
10am - 4:30pm
Sunday 1:30pm – 4:30pm

DEGREE OF DIFFICULTY
Easy

CONTACT
619.239.5548
www.timkenmuseum.org

The Timken Museum of Art is located in beautiful Balboa Park across from the international visitor's center. Here, visitors get the chance to see art from the extensive Putnam collection, comprised of European and America paintings and priceless Russian icons. Embracing the idea of sharing this fabulous collection with the public, the Timken doesn't charge for admission.

The Timken is rather small, yet the way the exhibits are setup give it the feel of a much larger space. Notable works include the1776 Benjamin West painting, "Fidelia and Speranza." The first American-born painter to study abroad, West's work reflects the classical sculptures and old masters he saw in Europe. The "Portrait of a Youth Holding an Arrow" by Giovanni Antonio Boltraffio, painted around 1500, is a stylized representation of the Greek god Apollo.

The Russian icons are wonderful examples of the art of the Eastern Orthodox Church. Blessed by priests for holy use, the images are of a sacred person or events during the year. In particular, the pieces on display were created for prayer and liturgical use in the church and home. The art itself is created out of metals, ivory, mosaic and even fresco. The common medium used for these pieces is tempera. The opportunity to see these priceless paintings in such an intimate setting is a rare treat.

TAKE THE TOUR

WHERE TO GO
2733 San Diego Avenue
Old Town San Diego State Park
San Diego, CA 92110

WHEN TO GO
Self-Guided Tours
10am - 5pm Daily

DEGREE OF DIFFICULTY
Easy

CONTACT
619.238.3929
www.wellsfargo.com

WELLS FARGO HISTORY MUSEUM

The Wells Fargo History Museum is part of the Old Town San Diego State Park, just a few miles from downtown. With one of the most famous names in American business, this tour relates the history of the expansion of the nation into the west as well as stories facts about California's gold rush, all told through the history of the country's once premiere delivery service and banking institution.

The museum explores what made the development of the West possible and how Wells Fargo, and banks in general, were instrumental in the success of this expansion. Once the California Gold Rush started, miners and the business that supported them needed a place to put their fortunes. Buying and selling gold, safekeeping of valuables and delivering letters is what made the company famous. During the 1860's Wells Fargo controlled the mail and transportation in the Western United States.

The museum gives visitors a chance to better understand how this banking institution grew, providing a valuable and reliable service for the growing nation. From the full size stagecoach parked in the front of the museum to the historic photographs of the drivers, visitors get to see for themselves the people and events that created this legacy. The Wells Fargo Museum is in a great place to start a day of touring. Once finished with the museum, visitors can step outside the door and take the guided tour of Old Town San Diego State Park.

CHINA RANCH

DESERT REGION

CHINA RANCH

The name "China Ranch" is thought to come from the man who originally owned the ranch. A Chinese man named Quon Sing or Ah Foo came to work at the ranch and made a name for himself by growing fruits and vegetables and raising meat for the local mining camps. As he grew the ranch, it became known as Chinaman's Ranch. However, a man named Morrison appeared around 1900 and ran the Chinese farmer off at gun point and claimed the ranch as his own. The owner changed, but the name stuck. Charles Brown Jr. and Bernice Sorrells, family of the venerable state Senator Charles Brown of Shoshone, purchased the property in 1970 and still own the property today.

The tour of China Ranch includes facts about date trees and farming in such an arid region. For example, the United States produces 60 million pounds of dates a year and an average tree produces 200 to 300 pounds of fruit a year. Commercial farms start work in early March and April when both male and female trees produce brown pods that mature to show a flower inside. The pods are combined for pollination through an interesting process that can be explored on the tour. By May the dates grow to the size of a marble and stalks have begun to grow. The flexible stalks are bent over and tied close to the ground. In late August, the dates are full-sized, but still green. Heavy paper wraps are placed over them to protect

TAKE THE TOUR

WHERE TO GO
Shoshone, CA 92384

WHEN TO GO
Self Guided Tours
9am -5pm Daily

DEGREE OF DIFFICULTY
Moderate to Difficult

CONTACT
760.852.4415
www.chinaranch.com

them from the elements and birds so they can ripen into a bright red or golden yellow color. From September through December, the fruit continues to ripen, turning to brown or black when ready to harvest.

After taking the farm tour it's worth the time to explore one of the hiking trails that begin outside the gift shop. All sorts of wildlife, including badgers, coyotes and foxes can be seen at different times along the trails. There are also more than 100 species of birds that make China Ranch their home can be observed around the ranch or on the trails. The more difficult Crack Trail leads to the Acme Siding, an ore-loading site, and stops at the Tonopah and Tidewater railroad that operated from 1905 to 1938. For those seeking a more leisurely, less strenuous stroll, a walk along the Old Spanish Trail is the ticket. Abandoned mines stand in silent testimony to the history of the area and can be found on several of the trails. The website is a great place to find more information about the hiking trails in the area.

Tours FOR FREE ™

ATLANTIS AQUARIUM
BEHIND THE SCENES TOUR

ETHEL M. CHOCOLATES

FLAMINGO HILTON
WILDLIFE HABITAT

LION HABITAT

MCCARRAN AVIATION
HISTORY MUSEUM

NATIONAL VITAMIN
COMPANY

RON LEE'S WORLD
OF CLOWNS

SHELBY CAR COMPANY

LAS VEGAS

ATLANTIC
AQUARIUM BEHIND
THE SCENES TOUR

TAKE THE TOUR

WHERE TO GO
Caesars Palace
3500 Las Vegas Boulevard
Las Vegas, NV 89109

WHEN TO GO
Guided Tours
Monday - Friday
1:15pm & 5:15pm

DEGREE OF DIFFICULTY
Easy

CONTACT
702.893.3807
www.caesarspalace.com

When people think of Las Vegas, an ocean is the last ing to come to mind. But the Atlantis Aquarium: ehind the Scenes Tour at the Caesars Palace will ange that. The Atlantis Aquarium is a beautiful 50,000-allon tank. The guided tour offers informative and teresting facts about the dozens of species of fish on site, the oceans they came om and the creation and maintenance of the aquarium. If you miss the guided ur, take time to stop by and watch the fish being d. The aquarium is a calming escape from the st pace of the city.

The circular tank contains more than 0 species of fish, from large sharks d sting rays to the smaller, olorful angel fish and porcupine sh. The aquarium handlers are sponsible for the health and elfare of these sometimes delicate nimals so they closely watch the condition of the ater, keep an eye out for signs of health problems with the fish and dive twice a day for feedings.

To find the tour, look for the large posted sign next to the tank. The aquarium handlers will be waiting for you at the indicated times. The tour begins downstairs under the tank where new fish are brought to be adapted to the aquarium. All the fish in the tanks are from the Caribbean. The process of adapting new fish to the tank is very important to the health of both the new fish and the controlled ecosystem created in the aquarium. The handlers are very careful about which species are added to the aquarium and the health of the fish. To keep a tight control on the aquarium, the handlers buy fish directly from the catchers who specialize in working with aquariums and then the fish are packed and flown directly to Caesars Palace. This ensures the fish are not mistreated or subjected to any toxins.

There are five tanks in this area, each with a different function. The first tank is the adapting tank. Here new arrivals are desensitized to humans before they are put into the main tank. This process is very important as the animals in the main tank are hand fed by divers, so they need to be comfortable around humans. The four other tanks in this area rotate so it is always a surprise as to what will be found in a given tank on a given day.

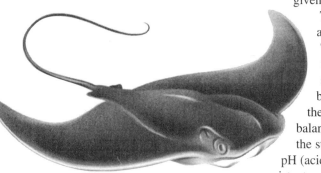

The tour proceeds to the aquarium cleaning systems. This is an elaborate process using multiple filtration systems and chemical balancing systems. Keeping the water in the tank clean and balanced is a primary concern of the staff. If the water is dirty, the pH (acidic level of the water) is not consistent or the water is too hot or cold, it stresses the fish and they could die. It's amazing how long it takes to change the pH or other conditions in a 50,000-gallon tank. Any problems that are left undetected or are not corrected immediately can lead to losses in the collection.

The next part is the best: the food. Since the fish live in Las Vegas, with buffets on every block, you can imagine that the food they get is just as good. When the tour guide opens up the freezer, it becomes clear just how well these fish eat. From frozen scallops and several varieties of fish to food pellets, it is clear the inhabitants of this aquarium are seriously pampered.

The final part of the tour is the educational room. Here, an outstanding aquarium that balances smaller fish with a wide variety of colorful corals and oddly shaped sponges is on display and is often used for demonstrations and lectures for school groups. A recurring theme is showing curious children just how fragile the ocean ecosystem is.

Visitors come away from this tour with interesting facts and information about fish and aquariums in general. It is clear that the people who care for the fish love their jobs and that enthusiasm makes the Atlantis Aquarium tour a fun and educational detour from the usual glitz and gambling of Las Vegas.

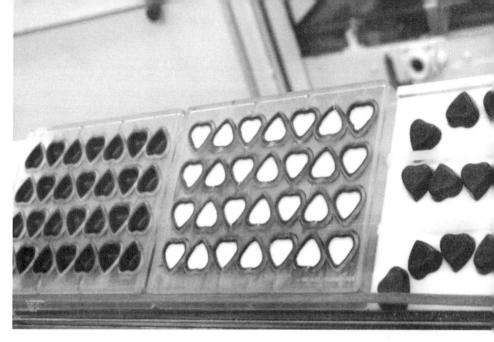

ETHEL M.
CHOCOLATES

TAKE THE TOUR

WHERE TO GO
2 Cactus Garden Drive
Henderson, NV 89014

WHEN TO GO
Self Guided Tour
8:30am - 7pm daily

DEGREE OF DIFFICULTY
Easy

CONTACT
702.435.2655
www.ethelm.com

Visitors to Ethel M. Chocolates are pleasantly overwhelmed in the parking lot by the wonderful scent of chocolate. Ethel M. is a large chocolate company with national catalog distribution, a great website and stores throughout Las Vegas and other states. This factory produces thousands of pounds of chocolate each year. Only minutes from the Las Vegas strip, this tour is a great chance to see how chocolates are made and to get a sample.

This self-guided tour follows the process of chocolate making from kettle to mold to fancy box. Large plate glass windows give a clear view of the process. Ethel M. makes more than 52 different flavors of chocolate, most of which are produced in this facility, but visitors will only see five or six kinds being made at a time. Beginning with the molding of the chocolate, the tour goes from the center of the chocolate piece to the outside cover. Examples of how different varieties of chocolates are made are placed in front of the windows and the process is clearly described. Above, video monitors show a short presentation on how the different pieces are made. All the machines that can be observed through the window are clearly labeled to make it easy to follow along with the video.

In the middle of the tour, visitors get the chance to actually see the process up close. Employees work a miniature production line to demonstrate how the candy is covered to create the perfect piece. While watching this process unfold, visitors can't help but marvel at how technical the candy making process has become.

Further down the line is the chocolate finishing section. There is a great deal of care to ensure the quality of the candy that is boxed and shipped to customers and retail outlets. The result of this attention can be tasted just around the corner where, at the end of the tour, a huge glass case full of chocolates awaits. From crème-filled pieces to solid milk chocolate, visitors can pick a piece of whatever their heart desires.

Before leaving Ethel M. Chocolates, visitors can take in two additional tours including the Living Machine and a beautiful botanical cactus garden. The Living

Machine is the first water recycling plant of its kind. Using Snails, microbes, plants and fish, wastewater is treated and converted to compost for use in agriculture. This acre of waste-consuming plants and animals contained in the tanks, marshes and reed beds is fascinating to learn about and important to the environment. Ethel M. Plant Manager Steven Clark predicts that this process contributes to saving up to 20,000 gallons of water a day; an important effort for a business located in a desert.

The tour of the botanical cactus garden is no less a treat. With the different types of cacti labeled, the chance to walk through and look at the varieties in one place is a great way to give that good chocolate some time to digest.

FLAMINGO HILTON WILDLIFE HABITAT

TAKE THE TOUR

WHERE TO GO
3555 Las Vegas Boulevard
Las Vegas, NV 89109

WHEN TO GO
Self-Guided Tours
Seven days a week

DEGREE OF DIFFICULTY
Easy

CONTACT
702.733.3111
www.flamingolasvegas.com

It is hard to think of penguins in the middle of the desert, but this is Las Vegas so it is not surprising to find the "well-dressed" birds showing off at the Flamingo Hilton. Open daily, the Flamingo Hilton Wildlife Habitat offers the chance to be entertained by these wild creatures. Open day and night, a stop at the habitat will fit any schedule.

Behind the hotel and casino of the Flamingo Hilton, a special area has been cultivated for the animals that call Las Vegas their new, high-class home. The main attraction is the penguins. Living it up in their specially chilled pool just outside the

hotel doors, these animals are more than happy to swim around and hang on the rocks while entertaining the guests who stop to watch.

A pathway divides the penguins and the flamingos. The stately elegance of the flamingo is quite extraordinary, not to mention colorful, as are the other birds that call the habitat home. The ponds and streams that run along the pathway are full of orange, black and white goldfish, adding to the wonderful setting of the habitat.

The animals are fed twice daily and visitors are encouraged to attend. As feeding times change, it is recommended to call ahead.

LION HABITAT

You probably already know about the lions from the films MGM produces. Before the movie, or even the previews, the lion's roar from the screen prepares the audience for the feature film. MGM Grand has taken that excitment one step further - they have made the roar live. Located in the center of the hotel, the Lion Habitat is a place to enjoy learning more about lions, lionesses and cubs as they roam only five feet from visitors. It is thrilling, especially when they roar.

Full-length windows enclose the habitat on three sides. On each window boards give explanations about the lions, their habitat and how they live - from the average weight of an adult to where they came from. Looking at the animals through the windows is interesting, but visitors need to go in to the glass viewing hallway to see the lions more closely. Here, the lions sit and play overhead. Looking up, the true size and strength of these mammals is apparent. Guides are on hand to answer questions and talk about fun facts. This adds a lot to the experience.

Further down the glass hall are the lion cubs. The size of a medium dog, these youngsters are more powerful than expected. That is why the trainers who work with them have to stay alert to keep from getting hurt. The opportunity to watch the handlers in action is fascinating.

The tour ends in a gift shop, but the lions are so fascinating you might want to go around again.

TAKE THE TOUR

WHERE TO GO
MGM Grand Hotel
3799 Las Vegas Boulevard
Las Vegas, NV 89109

WHEN TO GO
Self-Guided Tours
11am – 11pm daily

DEGREE OF DIFFICULTY
Easy

CONTACT
702.891.7777
www.mgmgrand.com

HOWARD W. CANNON AVIATION HISTORY MUSEUM

TAKE THE TOUR

WHERE TO GO
McCarran International Airport
Las Vegas, NV 89119

WHEN TO GO
Self-Guided Tour
Open Daily

DEGREE OF DIFFICULTY
Easy

CONTACT
702.261.5211

The gateway to Las Vegas, McCarran International Airport is used by nearly everyone visiting the city, but few wander upstairs to the aviation history museum. The museum does a good job of showing and telling the story of aviation history as well as offering a bird's eye view of how the city has grown.

Starting above the baggage claim area, hanging from the ceiling, is the small plane that was once used at the airport to deliver a handful of passengers per trip. Taking the escalators up, a full-size Cadillac used to shuttle passengers to and from the hotels downtown is also on display. This is a great place for a photo opportunity standing next to this gleaming ride, with the vintage plane in the background.

From the nostalgic to the contemporary, the exhibit covers World War II era planes and the use of planes in the region as Las Vegas developed. Also on display are relics from different individuals and companies who have used the airport.

Today the airport is internationally known and has more than 30 national and international airlines flying in and out daily. If you need to kill some time waiting for a delayed flight, take a look. The exhibits are open daily and are not far from the gates.

TAKE THE TOUR

WHERE TO GO
7440 S. Industrial Road,
Suite 210
Las Vegas, NV 89139

WHEN TO GO
Self-Guided Tour
Monday – Saturday
6am - 5pm
Sunday 6am – 3pm

DEGREE OF DIFFICULTY
Easy

CONTACT
702.269.9600
www.nationalvitamin.com

NATIONAL VITAMIN COMPANY

From A to Zinc, vitamins and minerals are essential compounds that keep our bodies functioning. The tour at the National Vitamin Company shows visitors how they put all those important nutrients into such small capsules.

The tour is self-guided and there are monitors describing every room along the large hallway. Taking as long as you like, you can watch the machinery in action and watch videos that explain the process step-by-step.

The most fascinating part of the tour is the manufacturing of soft gelatin capsules. The machinery makes large, continuous sheets of warm, light yellow gelatin used to coat the vitamins. Once the gelatin flows out of the main part of the machine, the gelatin coating is cut out, folded and the vitamin liquid is inserted, and the product sealed. The vitamins are then placed on sheets to be cooled and checked.

Next door to the gelatin manufacturing operation is the two-piece encapsulating process. Some vitamins come in capsules because they digest faster than tablets. It is impressive to watch a machine open each capsule, fill it with powdered form of the vitamins and put the cap back on, all in the flash of an eye. A window next to the encapsulating machine reveals a blender that looks like a cement truck rotating to combine the ingredients that will fill each capsule.

At the end of the tour, visitors are given a sample packet of vitamins and all the products made in the facility are available for purchase in the gift shop.

RON LEE'S WORLD OF CLOWNS

TAKE THE TOUR

WHERE TO GO
330 Carousel Parkway
Henderson, NV 89014

WHEN TO GO
Self-Guided Tours
Monday - Friday
8:30am - 3:30pm

DEGREE OF DIFFICULTY
Easy

CONTACT
702.434.1700
www.ronlee.com

Driving up the long driveway to Ron Lee's World of Clowns, you know you have the right place when you see the life-size clowns in the window of the large pink building. Ron Lee's World of Clowns is a tour that celebrates those silly, orange-haired people with the big shoes.

Ron Lee spent more than 25 years working as a professional artist and sculptor, but his real love was the circus. So he did what any obsessed joker would do, turned his affection into a business by creating the world's largest collection of clown figurines. Originally from Southern California, he and his family moved to Las Vegas where he creates 750 different designs of figurines. He estimates that two million of his clowns are now in homes around the world.

The entire tour focuses on how each figurine is made. The tour winds around the various artists and craftspeople while they are working. Between five and seven people contribute to making each figurine.

The tour starts at the painting station where identical figurines stand, lined on a table, waiting their turn to be painted and have final details added before being mounted on an onyx base. Winding around the hall, the tour covers the entire process start to finish. Each station has a video playing above so visitors can fully understand the process of making the clowns. The punch line of the tour is the shipping room where hundreds of figurines are prepared for shipping.

A gallery of clown art rounds out the tour and if any tickle your funny bone, they are available for purchase.

SHELBY AMERICAN

TAKE THE TOUR

WHERE TO GO
6755 Speedway Blvd
Las Vegas, NV 89115

WHEN TO GO
Guided Tours
Monday – Friday 10:30am

DEGREE OF DIFFICULTY
Easy

CONTACT
702.643.3000
www.shelbyamerican.com

Less than a mile from the Las Vegas Speedway, the Shelby Car Company is a tour no self-respecting, classic car enthusiast would miss. Mixing equal measures of history and assembly, visitors get the chance to see an American car manufacturer hard at work. Owned by legendary car designer Carroll Shelby, this tour offers the opportunity to see the classic design of the Cobra with modern construction, components and unbelievable power.

The tour begins in the museum with a guide talking about the engineering and details that made these muscle cars of the 60s and 70s the benchmark of performance for sports cars for years to come.

Each car Shelby makes is now custom ordered and the cars on display are all one of a kind.

The tour continues with a discussion of the different body types available, fiberglass and aluminum. Not as strong as aluminum, fiberglass is lighter, but most buyers prefer the traditional aluminum bodies over the fiberglass version (made by Nevada prison inmates). Approaching the production line, visitors get to see cars in various stages of assembly.

The cars are fully assembled, except for the engine. This is so buyers can choose the engine that best suits their taste. Shelby recommends different engines based on a buyer's driving skill and performance demands. Some of the machines can top 140 mph without even breaking a sweat, so new owners can also get high performance driving lessons to go with their new wheels.

Tours *FOR* **FREE**™

In this section you find a variety of listings for museums and other venues that normally charge an entry fee, but offer free admission on specified days during the year. There are numerous parades, community fairs and events that are perfect additions to vacations and outings. These listings will help fill the days with fun, free places to go and things to see and experience at no cost.

As with the tours listed in the book, it is best to call in advance to make sure that nothing has changed in these listings of events and free days.

FREE DAYS & FREE PLACES TO GO

OS ANGELES COUNTY MUSEUM OF ART

FREE Admission
The second Tuesday of every month.
5905 Wilshire Blvd
Los Angeles, CA 90036
323.932.5861
http://www.lacma.org/

From American art to Chinese and Korean art examples can be found here. The
Costume and Textile exhibits include over 50,000 items from 900 B.C. to present day.

HE LATINO BOOK AND FAMILY FESTIVAL

FREE Festival
October 13 and 14, 2002: Call or go online for future dates.
Los Angeles Convention Center
Los Angeles, California
760.434.7474
http://www.latinobookfestival.com/home/index.html

Celebrating Latino families, the festival welcomes the community to share
information, food and fun during this two day event.

IUSEUM OF CONTEMPORARY ART (MOCA)

FREE Admission
5pm to 8pm every Thursdays.
250 S Grand Ave,
Los Angeles, CA 90012
213.621.2766
http://www.moca.org/

IOCA AT THE GEFFEN CONTEMPORARY

FREE Admission
Every Thursday from 5pm to 8pm.
152 N Central Ave,
Los Angeles, CA 90013
213.626.6222
http://www.moca.org/

Located in the heart of Little Tokyo, this branch of MOCA was the original site
of the famous museum. The branch is known for its commitment to media and
the performing arts.

MOCA AT THE PACIFIC DESIGN CENTER

FREE Admission
5pm to 8pm every Thursday
8687 Melrose Avenue
West Hollywood, CA 90069
213.626.6222
http://www.moca.com/

Located in the Pacific Design Center, this location's exhibits emphasize architecture and design.

HOLLYWOOD & SAN FERNANDO VALLEY

ANNUAL NOHO THEATER AND ARTS FESTIVAL

FREE Show
Early June
NoHo Theater
Lankershim Blvd between Magnolia and Chandler
North Hollywood, California
Call for details and specific date 818.508.5155
http://www.1bc.com/vtl/default.htm

An annual event at the theater highlighting the culture and a taste of NoHo with original crafts and fine art. Call for exact days,

HOLLYWOOD CHRISTMAS PARADE

FREE Parade
December 1, 6-8 pm
Hollywood Boulevard starting at Mann's Theater
Hollywood, California
323.469.2337
http://www.hollywoodchristmas.com/

One of the most recognized parades in the country. Watch the Hoilday, traditional stories come alive on the streets of Hollywood. Catering to Santa's special day, you will also get a glimpse of a movie star or two on the floats that pass.

BANDS AT THE BOWL

FREE Performance
November 30, 9:30 am-Noon
Hollywood Bowl
Hollywood, California
323.469.2337
http://www.hollywoodchristmas.com/

Highlighting bands from across the country, this special concert brings the best together in the Holiday Bowl. For the grand finale all the musicians joining together for a holiday melody.

PASADENA & VICINITY

DOO DAH PARADE

FREE Admission
November 24
Raymond Avenue and Holly Street
Pasadena, California
 626.440.7379
http://pasadenadoodahparade.com

A crazy annual parade drawing the entire community together. More than 1,200 people parade in comical costumes during this festive morning.

PACIFIC ASIA MUSEUM

FREE Admission
Every third Saturday of the month.
46 N Los Robles Ave
Pasadena, CA 91101
626.449.2742
http://www.pacificasiamuseum.org/

Celebrating the diverse cultural heritage of Los Angeles, the museum displays artifacts, relics and works of art from all over Asia and the Pacific Islands.

KIDSPACE CHILDREN'S MUSEUM

FREE Admission
The last Monday of the month.
390 S El Molino Avenue
Pasadena, CA 91101
626.449.9143
http://www.kidspacemuseum.org/

Full of activities for children, the museum is best known for the Ant Wall. A jungle gym plant exclusively for kids with leaves spaced just far enough apart, children can climb up to the ceiling 20 feet above.

OLD PASADENA SUMMERFEST

FREE Event
May 25-27
Pasadena, California
626.797.6803
http://oldpasadenasummerfest.com/

Pasadena's special celebration of summer, this community festival features music, arts and crafts, food and sports.

SIERRA MADRE ART FAIR

FREE Event
May 18-19, 2002: Call or go online for future dates.
Memorial Park at 222 W. Sierra Madre Blvd.
Sierra Madre, California
626.355.7186
http://www.sierramadre.lib.ca.us/

 Near Pasadena, this fine art fair is a chance to see the splendor of the art community. Located at a park, kids are welcome to play on the playground.

FREE SUMMER CONCERTS IN CHACE PARK

FREE concerts
Thursday and Saturday nights, 7pm
13650 Mindanao Way
Marina Del Ray, California
310-305-9545
http://beaches.co.la.ca.us/BandH/Events/Main.asp#

At the presenting free concerts at Chace Park, you can listen to classical music is on Thursdays and Pops on Saturdays. All concerts will start at 7 p.m. to allow audiences to enjoy the sunset over the water.

2002 LOTUS FESTIVAL

FREE Festival
July 13, 2002 - 12:00 Noon to 9:30 pm
July14, 2002 - 12:00 Noon to 8:30 pm
Call or go online for future dates.
Echo Park
Los Angeles, California
213.485.1310
http://laparks.org/grifmet/lotus.htm

Coinciding with the blooming of the lotus flower in Los Angeles, the festival allows the public a sampling of uniquely Asian and Pacific Island customs and traditions.

HALLOWEEN & COSTUME CARNIVAL

FREE Event
Thursday, October 31, 2002: Call or go online for future dates.
6 PM - 12 Midnight
Santa Monica Boulevard
West Hollywood, California
310.289.2525

Drawing over 400,000 participants to Santa Monica Boulevard for food, merriment and costume contests, the festival is held annually on Halloween.

SOUTH COAST BOTANICAL GARDENS

FREE Admission
Third Tuesday of every month.
26300 S Crenshaw Boulevard
Palos Verdes Peninsula, CA 90274
310.544.6815
http://parks.co.la.ca.us/south_coast_botanic.html

Once a landfill, this 87-acre garden is a landscaper's paradise. Over 150,000 plants grow on the property and a variety of birds that are attracted to the area.

UCLA HAMMER MUSEUM

FREE Admission
Thursdays
10899 Wilshire Blvd
Los Angeles, CA 90024
310.443.7000
http://www.hammer.ucla.edu/

The Hammer Museum was designed by prominent New York architect Edward Larrabee Barnes, and opened to the public on November 28, 1990. UCLA started managing the museum on April 1, 1994. The museum has 14,000 feet of exhibition space for year round exhibits.

FOWLER MUSEUM OF CULTURAL HISTORY

FREE Admission
Thursday.
308 Charles E. Young Drive
Los Angeles, CA 90095
310.825.4361
http://www.fmch.ucla.edu/

The primary mission of the Fowler Museum is to present materials from Africa, Asia, Oceania, Native and Latin America. The collection also serves as a resource for students and faculty of UCLA.

JAPANESE AMERICAN NATIONAL MUSEUM

FREE Admission
Thursdays 5-7:30 pm
FREE Admission on the third Thursday every month
369 E 1st St
Los Angeles, CA 90012
213.625.0414
http://www.janm.org/

The only museum in the United States dedicated to sharing the experience of Japanese Americans, the doors of this institution opened in 1992. Promoting culture and understanding, the chance to see artifacts from the past as well as the challenges of the future should not be missed.

MUSEUM OF NEON ART

FREE Admission
Second Thursday of every month from 5pm to 8pm.
501 W Olympic Blvd
Los Angeles, CA 90015
213.489.9918
http://www.neonmona.org/

Founded in 1981, the museum offers visitors the opportunitiy to see the art of neon signs from around the country. This is one of the few collections of neon signs open to the public.

NATURAL HISTORY MUSEUM OF LOS ANGELES

FREE Admission
First Tuesday of every month.
In Exposition Park
900 Exposition Blvd
Los Angeles, CA 90007
213.763.3466
http://www.nhm.org/

The oldest and largest natural history museum in western America, guests will see actual dinosaur skeletons and the largest collection of gold on display in the United States. The museum has more than 33 million items on display.

ARBORETUM OF LOS ANGELES COUNTY

FREE Admission
Third Tuesday of every month.
301 North Baldwin Avenue
Arcadia, CA 91007
626.821.3222
http://www.arboretum.org/

The 127-acre grounds of the Arboretum are arranged primarily by geographic origins to easily walk around. Several original historical structures, wickiups, and Gabrieleno Indian structures may be seen as you tour the grounds.

GEORGE C. PAGE MUSEUM

FREE Admission
First Tuesday of every month
5801 Wilshire Blvd
Los Angeles, CA 90036
323.857.6311
http://www.tarpits.org

More than one million prehistoric specimens recovered from the asphalt deposits of the famous La Brea Tar Pits are the main attraction at the George C. Page Museum. Located in the heart of Los Angeles, the tar pits are only steps away from the museum.

ALHAMBRA SPRINGFEST

FREE Event
Saturday May 18th, 2002: Call or go online for future dates.
Main Street between Chapel and Fourth Street
626.282.5767
http://downtownalhambra.com

Sharing the Alhambra lifestyle, the community festival shares arts and crafts, food, a car show, entertainment and children's rides.

ANNUAL INTERNATIONAL FAMILY FESTIVAL

FREE Festival
August 3 – 5, 2002: Call or go online for future dates.
700 W. Manchester Ave.
Westchester, California
310.202.2850
http://www.laparks.org/int_festival/home.htm

Celebrating the culturally diverse residents of Los Angeles, the entire family is invited to share in the fun, enjoyment and learning of the many cultures living in Los Angeles. The 3-day special event celebrates by providing activities and programs with an international flavor appropriate for all ages.

PILGRIM THANKSGIVING FESTIVAL

FREE Festival
November 8 and 9, 2002: Call or go online for future dates.
Pilgrim Place
Claremont, California
909.621.9581
http://www.pilgrimplace.org/Festival.html

Reaching out to the community, the Pilgrim Place Retirement Village holds a Craft Fair & Bazaar. Making it appropriate for all ages, children's activities including rides, crafts and treats are available for the kids to enjoy.

PALM SPRINGS DESERT MUSEUM

FREE Admission
First Friday of every month.
101 Museum Drive
Palm Springs, CA 92262
760.325.7186
http://www.psmuseum.org/

Established in 1938, the museum promotes art, natural science and performing arts in the desert communities. The permanent art collection focuses on contemporary California, classic Western American, Native American and Pre Columbian art.

HUNTINGTON LIBRARY, ART GALLERIES AND BOTANICAL GARDENS

FREE Admission
First Thursday of every month
1151 Oxford Rd
San Marino, CA 91108
626.405.2141
http://www.huntington.org/

A large collection of 18th and 19th century art is on display inside for guests to view. Outside the equivalent of Eden is on display with the elegant thematic gardens around the stylish mansion.

RAYMOND M. ALF MUSEUM

FREE Admission
Every Wednesday
1175 W Baseline Road
Claremont, CA 91711
909.624.2798
http://www.alfmuseum.org/

Launched in 1937, the museum has hosted 250,000 guests and has given them a look at fossils and dinosaurs. The two large exhibit halls, the Hall of Life and the Hall of Footprints are arranged to show archaeological artifacts from around the world.

ORANGE COUNTY

GOGH VAN ORANGE ART AND MUSIC FESTIVAL

FREE festival
Early June
Historic Orange Plaza
Orange, California
714.538.3581

The annual Gogh Van Orange Art & Music Festival offers an exhibit of works by more than 50 Southern California artists and free performances by noted jazz, blues, and swing musicians. A children's area providing a chalk art competition, plays, & dance performances will delight the youngsters.

TUSTIN TILLER DAYS

FREE event
October 12-13, 2002: Call or go online for future dates.
Tustin, California
714.573.3334
http://tustintillerdays.org/

Beginning in 1957, the celebration of Orange County's agricultural heritage is good fun within the community. It is also an opportunity for local nonprofit groups to raise funds.

CONCERTS IN THE PARK

FREE Concerts
June 19; 26; July 17; 24; 31; August 7; 14
Hart Park
Orange, California
714.744.7286
http://cityoforange.org

Hearing sounds of the summer, the outdoor music series is a chance to watch the sunset and relax to smooth music. Picnic baskets are welcome.

FIESTA STREET FESTIVAL

FREE Festival
August 11
Ave Del Mar
San Clemente, California
949.492.1131
http://scchamber.com

The excitement of the San Clemente community brings people to the festival. Highlights include a 5k walk/run, music, games, and exhibits.

CARNEGIE ART MUSEUM

FREE Admission
Fridays from 3 to 5pm
424 South 'C' Street
Oxnard, CA 93030
805.385.8157
http://www.vcnet.com/carnart/default.html

A collection of art to share with the community, the museum has a distinguished reputation for covering works from film, video, American art, French Impressionist and Post-Impressionist paintings. The Heinz Architectural Center, opened in 1993, is dedicated to architectural drawings and models.

FRENCH FESTIVAL

FREE Festival
July 13 and 14, 2002: Call or go online for future dates.
Oak Park
Santa Barbara, California
805.564.7274
http://www.frenchfestival.com/

Largest French celebration in the Western United States, guests can learn more about France. The highlights include distinguished French food, music, dance, and a poodle parade. Non-stop entertainment is provided on three stages.

OXNARD SALSA FESTIVAL

FREE Festival
July 27 and 28, 2002: Call or go online for future dates.
Plaza Park
5th & B Streets
Oxnard, California
805.385.7545
 http://www.oxnardtourism.com/salsafestival.html

A taste of Mexico may be enjoyed at Plaza Park. Salsa tasting, salsa music, salsa dancing, international foods, and marketplace vendors will be available to explore.

ANNUAL VILLAGE KITE FESTIVAL

FREE Festival
Mid May
Harbor Village
Ventura, California
805.648.2875

Celebrating kite flying, Harbor Village is converted into a Kiteport. Hundreds of kites from the diamond kites to the box kites will take to the sky.

PORT HUENEME HARBOR DAYS FESTIVAL AND PARADE

FREE Festival
October 5 and 6, 2002: Call or go online for future dates.
Hueneme Beach - Surfside Drive at Ventura Road
Port Hueneme, California
805.487.4470
www.harbordays.org

Honoring the harbor that flows to the ocean, the two day festival is in its 46th season. From a car show to kite displays and music, from food, to an film festival it is not to be missed.

CALIFORNIA AVOCADO FESTIVAL

FREE Festival
October 5 and 6, 2002: Call or go online for future dates.
Linden Ave
Carpinteria, California
805.684.0038

Focusing on the fruit with the green insides, the annual festival is a chance to see one of the biggest bowls of guacamole anywhere. Try avocado ice cream, steak sandwichs with guacamole and avocado brownies.

FILLMORE ORANGE FESTIVAL

FREE Festival
May 4 and 5, 2002: Call or go online for future dates.
330 A Central Avenue
Fillmore, California
805.524.0351
http://www.fillmoreca.com/

One of the Santa Clara River Valley's largest products, the orange is honored during the last weekend in May. With a wealth of citrus groves only a stone's throw away, you can enjoy a slice of fruit and the festival.

SAN DIEGO ZOO

FREE DAY
First Monday of October
2920 Zoo Drive
San Diego, CA 92101
619.234.3153
http://www.sandiegozoo.org/

Home to 6,500 birds, mammals, and reptiles and easily as many exotic plants, guests may explore a world without man's intervention. The hippo beach is a favorite of tourists.

SAN DIEGO WILD ANIMAL PARK

FREE Day
May – call for details
15500 San Pasqual Valley Road
Escondido, CA
619.234.6541
http://www.sandiegozoo.org/wap/homepage.php3

Dedicated to the preservation and protection of endangered animals, the 2,200 acre reserve is a favorite of locals. The bird and elephant show is not to be missed.

MUSEUM OF CONTEMPORARY ART

FREE Admission
First Sunday and third Thursday of every month.
700 Prospect Street
La Jolla, CA 92037
858.454.3541
http://www.mcasandiego.org/

Housed in the Ellen Browning Scripp's House, the permanent collection is full of 20th Century works in a variety of media. The Garden Gallery is a must see as the outside grounds are home to exceptional sculptures and other art.

FIREHOUSE MUSEUM

FREE Admission
First Thursday of every month.
1572 Columbia Street
San Diego, CA 92101
619.232.3473

In the middle of Little Italy, this museum is located in a real firehouse. The equipment and exhibits are testaments to the men and women who dedicate their lives to safety in the danger of flames.

SAN DIEGO NATURAL HISTORY MUSEUM

FREE Admission
First Tuesday of every month
1788 El Prado
Balboa Park
San Diego, CA 92101
619.232.3821
http://www.sdnhm.org/

The museum is housed in a Spanish Colonial architecture inspired building of Balboa Park. Museum exhibits focus on the natural history of Southern and Baja California. Guests can't miss the crack in the floor of the atrium, a reproduction of the San Andreas Fault.

REUBEN H. FLEET SCIENCE CENTER

FREE Admission
First Tuesday of every month
1875 El Prado
Balboa Park
San Diego, CA 92101
619.238.1233
http://www.rhfleet.org/

A kid's favorite place, this center will give your family hands-on access to science. Exploring exhibits based on everyday life, the Center provides understanding and enjoyment of science and technology

SAN DIEGO MODEL RAILROAD MUSEUM

FREE Admission
First Tuesday of every month
1649 El Prado
Balboa Park
San Diego, CA 92101
619.696.0199
http://www.sdmodelrailroadm.com/

Home of the largest indoor model railroad display in the world, the museum has hosted over 2 million visitors. Showing some of California's railroads in miniature models, the heritage of railroading is shared to educate the public.

MUSEUM OF PHOTOGRAPHIC ARTS

FREE Admission
Second Tuesday of every month
1649 El Prado
Balboa Park
San Diego, CA 92101
619.238.7559
http://www.mopa.org/

Five galleries of exhibit space along with a naturally lit atrium highlights photographs housed at the museum. Focusing on the San Diego community, a large portion of photographs displayed were taken by Latin American artists.

MINGEI INTERNATIONAL FOLK ART MUSEUM

FREE Admission
Third Tuesday of every month
1439 El Prado
Balboa Park
San Diego, CA 92101
619.239.0003
http://www.mingei.org/

Folk Art from 83 countries, over 11,000 pieces, are part of the museum's permanent collection on display for guests to view. Traditional and contemporary, the exhibits are accompanied by music of the region of which the items are displayed.

SAN DIEGO MUSEUM OF ART

FREE Admission
Third Tuesday of every month
1450 El Prado
Balboa Park
San Diego, CA 92101
619.232.7931
http://www.sdmart.org/

Known to the locals as 'The Fine Arts Gallery" the permanent collection of this museum spans the American and European works to Chinese art,. The museum opened in 1927 and currently houses over 3,000 Western works on paper.

SAN DIEGO MUSEUM OF MAN

FREE Admission
Third Tuesday of every month
1350 El Prado
Balboa Park
San Diego, CA 92101
619.239.2001
http://www.museumofman.org/

The permanent collection of the museum is a major resource for the San Diego community. Exploring the human life cycle, guests can study the Maya, Egypt and the Kumeyaay Indians of San Diego.

SAN DIEGO HALL OF CHAMPIONS
– SPORTS MUSEUM

FREE Admission
Fourth Tuesday of every month
2131 Pan American Plaza
Balboa Park
San Diego, CA 92101
619.234.2544
http://www.sandiegosports.org/

Housed in the renovated Federal Building in Balboa Park, the museum focuses on Sports of San Diego and world-wide. The 70,000 square foot facility has three floors of exhibits encouraging guests to be interact as well as observe.

SAN DIEGO AUTOMOTIVE MUSEUM

FREE Admission
Fourth Tuesday of every month
2080 Pan American Plaza
Balboa Park
San Diego, CA 92101
619.231.2886
http://www.sdautomuseum.org/

Opening in December of 1988, the Museum houses over 80 vintage vehicles. From Automobiles to motorcycles, the opportunity to reflect on cruising when guests were youngsters is what thousands do yearly. The museum hosts special exhibits such as 50's Fantasia during the year.

CAJON CLASSIC CRUISE AND CAR SHOW

FREE Event
April 3- October 30
Wednesdays, 6:00pm-9:00pm
Main Street
El Cajon, California
619.401.8858
http://downtownelcajon.com/events.html

The largest weekly classic car show in Southern California takes place in El Cajon. Free to view the speed demons, the car show has a street fair flavor, features over 300 race cars, and specialty cars.

HOMETOWN HOLIDAYS

FREE Event
December 7, 2002: Call or go online for future dates.
Prescott Promenade
El Cajon, California
619.401.8858
http://downtownelcajon.com/events.html

A community holiday event celebrating the Christmas season the celebration offers food, music, dance, crafts, caroling and fun for the fun entire family. Over 10,000 Christmas revelers, mostly locals, enjoy visiting with neighbors during the holidays.

Hollywood Walk of Stars 28

Hotel del Coronado 127

Jet Propulsion Laboratory................42

Karpeles Manuscript
    Library Museum 71

Krispy Kreme Donuts.........................29

La Brea Tar Pits 11

Lawrence Welk Museum 112

Lincoln Memorial Shrine...................89

Lion Habitat 150

Long Beach Airport 57

Los Angeles City Hall 12

Los Angeles Farmers Market 13

Los Angeles Maritime Museum 58

Los Angeles Performing
    Arts Theater..................................14

Los Angeles Public Library 15

Los Angeles Temple..........................59

Los Angeles Times Editorial Tour......17

Los Angeles Times Olympic
    Plant Tour 18

Lummis House 60

March AFB Field Museum.................90

Marine Mammal Care Center
    at Fort MacArthur.........................61

McCarran Aviation
    History Museum 151

Museum of Contemporary Art
    Downtown 128

National RV Factory Tour..............114

National Vitamin Company 152

Old Town San Diego State
    Historical Park 129

Olivas Adobe 72

Orange County Performing
    Arts Center....................................98

Orange County Register...................99

Orcutt Ranch Horticulture
    Center 30

Orfila Vineyards................................115

Oxnard Heritage Square 73

Rancho Los Alamitos.........................62

Red Tile Tour 74

Ron Lee's World of Clowns............153

Salk Institute for Biological
    Studies 131

San Antonio Winery..........................20

San Diego Mineral and
    Gem Society...............................132

San Diego Union Tribune 133

Santa Barbara Airport......................75

MOTHER GOOSE PARADE

FREE Parade
Sunday before Thanksgiving
El Cajon, California
619.444.8712
http://www.mothergooseparade.com/

A Downtown El Cajon holiday tradition for more than 50 years, attracting more than 250,000 visitors. Featuring major floats and participants, it is the second largest parade West of the Mississippi River honoring the great Mother Goose.

BUDS 'N BLOOMS

FREE Festival
May 1-31
Balboa Park
San Diego, California
619.239.0512
http://balboapark.org

Gathering for a botanical celebration in Balboa Park, guests enjoy the great outdoors and the fruits of the ground. Arranging garden tours and exhibits for the gardener while the rest of the family can enjoy musical and dramatic presentations and children's activities.

NORTH PARK SPRING FESTIVAL

FREE Festival
May 19, 2002: Call or go online for future dates.
North Park
San Diego, California
619.294.2501
http://www.northparkmainstreet.com/Sprngfs/spfst2002.htm

Celebrating Spring weather and all the beauty of the community, locals enjoy the opportunity to get out and enjoy the day at this festival. Performances and food bring the locals back year after year.

19TH ANNUAL LATIN AMERICAN FESTIVAL

FREE Festival
August 2-4, 2002: Call or go online for future dates.
Old San Diego State Park
San Diego, California
619.296.3161
http://bazaardelmundo.com

This yearly festival features artist demonstrations and exhibits from Mexico, Guatemala, Peru and Panama. Hosting a view of Latin American crafts, demonstrations, entertainment and food booths guests are sure to leave with a better understanding Latin culture.

INTERNATIONAL FRIENDSHIP FESTIVAL

FREE Festival
September 21 and 22
El Cajon Civic Center
El Cajon, California
619.441.1753
http://ci.el-cajon.ca.us/

Spotlighting the strength in international cultures, this is a family event with children's activities including powwow, ethnic foods, arts and crafts, heritage displays, entertainment and fine arts exhibit.

SAN DIEGO EAST COUNTY FLEET WEEK CELEBRATION

FREE Festival
October
Gillespie Field
El Cajon, California
619.445.0180
http://visitsandiegoeast.com

Honoring those who work in the military and their families, this celebration takes place at the Gillespie Field. Aircraft will be on display, live entertainment, and a children's festival. The finale of the celebration is a fireworks show.

CHALK "LA STRADA"

FREE Festival
October 19 and 20, 2002: Call or go online for future dates.
Little Italy District
San Diego, California
1.877.DO.CHALK
http://www.chalklastrada.com

 A unique Italian streetpainting festival where you can see art in the making and walk on it. Over 125 artists participate in the 2 day festival. Using chalk the sidewalks will fill with vivid images of contemporary and classic images.

INTERNATIONAL FRIENDSHIP FESTIVAL

FREE Festival
4th Weekend in September
Saturday 10am-10pm, Sunday Noon-6pm
200 East Main Street
El Cajon, California
619.441.1753
http://www.ci.el-cajon.ca.us/

 Celebrating the community and its culture, this annual event has been attended since 1990. Celebrate over 60 different ethnic groups from the community through delicious food, crafts and traditional entertainment.

LAS VEGAS ART MUSEUM

FREE Admission
First Tuesday of every month
9600 W Sahara Ave
Las Vegas, NV 89117
702.360.8000
http://www.lastplace.com/EXHIBITS/LVAM/

Catering to the community, the museum's collection enlightens and enriches through fine arts. Changing exhibits include one-artist shows and collections from around the country.

BELLAGIO'S BOTANICAL GARDENS

FREE Admission
Daily
Bellagio Resort
3600 Las Vegas Blvd South
Las Vegas, Nevada
702.693.7111
http://www.bellagio.com/

Over 100 horticulturalists cater to the conservatory displaying 7,500 plants trees and flowers. Elegant and elaborate, the bright atrium is changed six to eight times a year to reflecting the seasons.

FOUNTAINS AT BELLAGIO

FREE Show
3 p.m. to midnight
Bellagio Resort
3600 Las Vegas Blvd South
Las Vegas, Nevada
702.693.7111
http://www.bellagio.com/

Choregraphed to songs, the fountains spew water from the lake in front of the Bellagio. To get a perfect show every evening 1,200 nozzles and 4,500 lights are used. The songs vary depending on the time of the year.

FALL OF ATLANTIS SHOW
AT CAESARS FORUM SHOPS

Hourly animatronic show
10 a.m. to 11 p.m
Forum Shops at Caesars Palace
3570 Las Vegas Blvd South
Las Vegas, Nevada
702.731.7110
http://www.caesarspalace.com/

Using electronic figures, the show is a reenactment of the mythological fight when the children of Atlas fight for control of Atlantis. The show starts promptly on the hour and fascinates guests with lights, smoke and sounds.

COURT JESTER'S STAGE

FREE Magic Show
10 – 10 daily
Excalibur Hotel
3850 Las Vegas Boulevard South
Las Vegas, Nevada
702.597.7777
http://www.excaliburlasvegas.com/
Entertaining guests with the thrill of magic and juggling, the center stage reveals the best of the sorcerer's tricks. Different performers entertain daily.

DRAGON BATTLE AT EXCALIBUR

FREE Show
Hourly dusk – 12am
Excalibur Hotel
3850 Las Vegas Boulevard South
Las Vegas, Nevada
702.597.7777
http://www.excaliburlasvegas.com/
Saving the day by battling a glary eyed dragon, Merlin's magic is shown to those who gather outside. Watching the dragon challenge the sorcerer, guests can see the exciting show on the hour.

FREMONT STREET EXPERIENCE

FREE Show
Dusk to midnight
25 Fremont Street
Las Vegas, NV 89101
702.678.5777

The canopy above Fremont Street will entertain you in seconds. Making noise using the 540,000 watt sound system plus you will be able to see clearly with the $70 million light canopy to find an experience unmatched.

MARJORIE BARRICK MUSEUM OF NATURAL HISTORY

FREE Admission
8 a.m. - 4:45 p.m., Mon. - Fri
10 a.m. - 2 p.m., Saturday
4505 S. Maryland Pkwy.
Las Vegas, NV 89154
702.895.3381
http://hrcweb.lv-hrc.nevada.edu/

Founded in 1969, the museum focuses on native cultures of the Southwest and Central Americas. Exploring the history of Las Vegas, building of Hoover Dam as well as understanding the Mojave Desert.

WORLD'S LARGEST PERMANENT CIRCUS

FREE Show
Circus Circus Hotel
702.734.0410
http://www.circuscircus.com/

Performing every half hour, circus entertainers don their makeup and amuse guests with their tricks. From the flying trapeze to plates rotating upon a stick, the show must go on.

TIGER HABITAT AT THE MIRAGE

FREE viewing
Open Daily
The Mirage
3400 Las Vegas Blvd South
Las Vegas, Nevada
702.791.7444
http://www.themirage.com/

Siegfried and Roy's Tigers are found in their million dollar habitat at the Mirage. A pool, waterfalls and guests can be found at this popular attraction.

THE VOLCANO

FREE Show
Every 15 minutes
Dusk until midnight
The Mirage
3400 Las Vegas Blvd South
Las Vegas, Nevada
702.791.7444
http://www.themirage.com/

The Volcano on the Las Vegas Strip erupts on a regular schedule into the night sky over 100 feet above the water. Once the eruption begins, the lagoon catches fire as guests watch a replica of Mother Nature in action.

PIRATE BATTLE AT TREASURE ISLAND

FREE Show
5:30 – 10pm, every 90 minutes
Treasure Island
3300 Las Vegas Blvd South
Las Vegas, Nevada
1.800.288.7206
http://www.treasureisland.com/

Battling the seas nightly, the ships Hispaniola and HMS Pinafore can be seen in the front of Treasure Island. Spewing insults, throwing men overboard and shooting fireworks, the entire show is watched safely from the shores.

MASQUERADE VILLAGE AT THE RIO

FREE Show
3:30, 4:30, 5:30, 7, 8, 9 and 10 p.m. daily.
3700 West Flamingo Rd.
Las Vegas, NV 89103
(702) 252-7777

Taking to the sky, the party and parade at the Rio is an exciting Masquerade Show. Mimes, acrobats and entertainers mingle with guests as dancers perform choreographed dances to music.

TOURS BY NAME

Antique Gas and Steam Engine Museum......103

Arco Olympic Center......121

Atlantis Aquarium Behind the Scenes Tour......145

Avila Adobe 3

Balboa Park......123

Banning Residence Museum 47

Bates Nut Farm......105

Bell Gardens 106

Bell of Friendship 49

Bernardo Winery 126

Buck Knives......124

Buena Vista Audubon Nature Center 107

Bungalow Heaven landmark Tour .41

Cabrillo Marine Aquarium 50

California Museum of Photography......83

California Science Center......5

California Surf Museum 108

Callaway Golf......109

Callaway Golf......110

Casa de Tortuga 51

Channel Islands Mainland Visitors Center......67

Chapalita Tortilla 6

China Ranch 141

Crystal Cathedral 53

Drum Barracks Civil War Museum...54

El Presidio de Santa Barbara......69

El Pueblo de Los Angeles 7

Ethel M Chocolates......147

Fillmore Fish Hatchery......70

Flamingo Hilton Wildlife Habitat....149

Fleetwood RV......85

Frederick's of Hollywood Lingerie Museum......25

Gallup & Stribling's Orchid Farm.........

Getty Center......56

Goodwill Industries......8

Gordon Howard Museum Complex 26

Graber Olive House......86

Grand Central Market 10

Guide Dogs of America......27

Heritage Hill Historical Park 97

Historical Glass Museum 88

Santa Barbara County
    Courthouse 76

Santa Barbara Historical
    Museum..77

Santa Barbara Winery......................78

Shelby American 154

SilverCrest Homes 91

Summers Past Farms.......................135

Taylor Guitars.................................136

Taylor Made Adidus Golf...............116

The Nethercutt Collection 31

The Nethercutt Museum 32

The Old Mill......................................44

The Road to Hollywood 34

The Timken Museum of Art 137

Ventura Historic Walking Tour 79

Wayfarers Chapel 64

Wells Fargo History Museum............21

Wells Fargo History Museum..........138

William S. Hart Museum....................35

Winchester Cheese 118

Witch Creek Winery.........................80

Workman and Temple Family
    Homestead Museum..................93

AGRICULTURE

Antique Gas and Steam Engine
    Museum......................................103

Bates Nut Farm...............................105

Bell Gardens 106

China Ranch 141

Fillmore Fish Hatchery......................70

Gallup & Stribling's Orchid Farm.........

Graber Olive House..........................86

Los Angeles Farmers Market 13

Orcutt Ranch Horticulture Center ..30

Rancho Los Alamitos.......................62

Summers Past Farms.......................135

Winchester Cheese 118

ANIMAL TOURS

Atlantis Aquarium Behind
    the Scenes Tour.........................145

Bates Nut Farm...............................105

Buena Vista Audubon
    Nature Center 107

Cabrillo Marine Aquarium 50

Casa de Tortuga 51

Fillmore Fish Hatchery........................70

Flamingo Hilton Wildlife Habitat....149

Guide Dogs of America....................27

Lion Habitat 150

Marine Mammal Care Center
    at Fort MacArthur........................61

William S. Hart Museum....................35

CRAZY GOOD FUN

Cabrillo Marine Aquarium 50

Casa de Tortuga 51

Ethel M Chocolates.........................147

Flamingo Hilton Wildlife Habitat....149

Frederick's of Hollywood
    Lingerie Museum..........................25

Hollywood Walk of Stars 28

Krispy Kreme Donuts.........................29

Lion Habitat 150

National Vitamin Company 152

Ron Lee's World of Clowns.............153

Taylor Guitars....................................136

The Road to Hollywood 34

EDUCATIONAL

Long Beach Airport 57

Los Angeles Times Editorial Tour......17

Los Angeles Times Olympic
    Plant Tour 18

Marine Mammal Care Center
    at Fort MacArthur........................61

Old Town San Diego State
    Historical Park 129

Orange County Performing
    Arts Center...................................98

Orange County Register.................99

San Diego Mineral and
    Gem Society...............................132

San Diego Union Tribune 133

Santa Barbara Airport 75

Santa Barbara Historical Museum ..77

Wells Fargo History Museum............21

Wells Fargo History Museum..........138

William S. Hart Museum....................35

GREAT FOR KIDS

Arco Olympic Center.....................121

Atlantis Aquarium Behind the
    Scenes Tour.................................145

Bates Nut Farm...............................105

Buena Vista Audubon
    Nature Center 107

Cabrillo Marine Aquarium 50

California Science Center.................5

Casa de Tortuga 51

Chapalita Tortilla 6

Ethel M Chocolates........................147

Flamingo Hilton Wildlife Habitat....149

Getty Center....................................56

Gordon Howard Museum
    Complex 26

Krispy Kreme Donuts.........................29

Lion Habitat....................................150

Long Beach Airport 57

Old Town San Diego State
    Historical Park 129

Santa Barbara Airport 75

The Road to Hollywood 34

Wells Fargo History Museum 21

Wells Fargo History Museum 138

William S. Hart Museum....................35

HISTORICAL

Antique Gas and Steam
    Engine Museum.........................103

Avila Adobe 3

Balboa Park.....................................123

Bell of Friendship 49

China Ranch 141

Drum Barracks Civil
    War Museum 54

El Presidio de Santa Barbara...........69

El Pueblo de Los Angeles 7

Gordon Howard
    Museum Complex.......................26

Heritage Hill Historical Park 97

Historical Glass Museum 88

Los Angeles Maritime Museum 58

March AFB Field Museum 90

Old Town San Diego State
    Historical Park 129

Olivas Adobe 72

Orcutt Ranch Horticulture
    Center 30

Oxnard Heritage Square 73

Rancho Los Alamitos.......................62

Santa Barbara County
    Courthouse 76

Santa Barbara Historical
    Museum...77

Ventura Historic Walking Tour 79

William S. Hart Museum....................35

Workman and Temple Family
    Homestead Museum 93

MUSEUMS

Antique Gas and Steam
    Engine Museum.........................103

Banning Residence Museum 47

California Surf Museum 108

Drum Barracks Civil War Museum...54

El Presidio de Santa Barbara...........69

El Pueblo de Los Angeles 7

Frederick's of Hollywood
    Lingerie Museum 25

Getty Center 56

Gordon Howard Museum
    Complex 26

Heritage Hill Historical Park 97

Historical Glass Museum 88

Karpeles Manuscript
    Library Museum 71

Lawrence Welk Museum 112

Lincoln Memorial Shrine...................89

Los Angeles Maritime Museum 58

Lummis House 60

March AFB Field Museum 90

McCarran Aviation
    History Museum 151

Old Town San Diego State
    Historical Park 129

Olivas Adobe 72

Santa Barbara Historical
    Museum...77

The Nethercutt Museum 32

Wells Fargo History Museum 21

Wells Fargo History Museum 138

William S. Hart Museum....................35

Workman and Temple Family
    Homestead Museum 93

TOTALLY CALIFORN

Balboa Park.....................................123

Bell of Friendship 49

Bungalow Heaven
    landmark Tour.............................41

California Science Center.................5

Casa de Tortuga 51

Channel Islands Mainland
    Visitors Center..............................67

Getty Center.....................................56

Graber Olive House.........................86

Grand Central Market 10

Guide Dogs of America...................27

Hollywood Walk of Stars 28

Hotel del Coronado 127

La Brea Tar Pits 11

Los Angeles Public Library 15

Los Angeles Times Editorial Tour......17

Los Angeles Times Olympic
    Plant Tour 18

Old Town San Diego State
    Historical Park 129

Orange County Register..................99

San Diego Union Tribune 133

Santa Barbara County
    Courthouse 76

Taylor Guitars..................................136

The Nethercutt Collection 31

Winchester Cheese 118

Callaway Golf.................................109

WINERIES

Bernardo Winery 126

Orfila Vineyards...............................115

San Antonio Winery 20

Santa Barbara Winery......................78

Witch Creek Winery.........................80

After twelve years as a literary agent and successfully helping many authors get their books published, Jodi Jill has moved on to being a full time author and promoter of her Quit Whining and Read! literacy program.

Tours For Free California is the second in the series. This edition shares Jodi's love of Southern California and best of all how others can get the most out of their trave dollar.

She is the creator to the Quit Whining and Read! Literacy program where she promotes literacy through art, information and making donations to literacy programs. The quitwhining.com website and her monthly newsletter "Make Words Work" has become an important part of promoting and encouraging literacy. Jill is the author of five other books, including Tours Fro Free Colorado, the popular Postmark Loveland and anthologies of her nationally syndicated puzzle Brain Baffler. Her love of puzzles led to her founding National Puzzle day, which is celebrated every January.

NOTES/TRAVEL LOG

NOTES/TRAVEL LOG

NOTES/TRAVEL LOG

NOTES/TRAVEL LOG

NOTES/TRAVEL LOG

NOTES/TRAVEL LOG

FREE TOURS
GO!

Grab the guidebook that gets you there for FREE

Tours For Free books are packed full of fun, entertaining, and educational tours.

From Candy Factories to wineries, newspapers to dinosaur tracks, guitars to golf clubs, these handy guides have something for everyone.

Whether you are traveling or if you live in the region – the Tours For Free books are a must have.

■ A fantastic way to stretch your vacation dollar

■ Perfect for entertaining visitors from out of town

■ Ideal for weekend trips that don't cost a dime

■ Wonderful for finding things to entertain the kids during the summer

TOUR FREE IN

Colorado
Southern California & Las Vegas
Coming October 2002
New York
Coming February 2003
Northern California

WWW.TOURSFORFREE.COM